ACADEMIA LUNARE

Gendering Time, Timing Gender

*The Deconstruction of Gender in
Time Travel Fiction*

I0134921

P.M. Biswas

Academia
Lunare
LUNA PRESS
PUBLISHING

Cover Image © Zamurovic Photography/Shutterstock.com
Text © P.M. Biswas 2021

First published by Luna Press Publishing, Edinburgh, 2021

www.lunapresspublishing.com

ISBN-13: 978-1-913387-35-8

*To Jane Messer, without whom
this book would not exist.*

CONTENTS

INTRODUCTION

A Journey Through Time and Gender

I eliminated gender to find out what was left. Whatever
was left would be, presumably, simply human.
— Ursula K. Le Guin, 'Is Gender Necessary? Redux.'

Topic and Scope

*Gendering Time, Timing Gender: The Deconstruction of
Gender in Time Travel Fiction* is a book that investigates
how time travel has been used to deconstruct gender and
sex in speculative fiction. Specifically, it investigates
how the dismantling of the past/future binary is utilised
in the dismantling of the male/female gender binary in
three different time travel narratives: *Orlando* by Virginia
Woolf, 'All You Zombies' by Robert A. Heinlein, and *The
Unintentional Time Traveler* by Everett Maroon.

All three works feature protagonists whose gender
identities are inextricably bound with time itself. As they
move through time, their sex and gender identity changes.
Time and gender are depicted as non-binary, with society
imposing a socially-constructed binary on what transcends
binaries altogether. The narratological shifts involved in
the representation of time travel create a deconstructive
counter-dialogic against heteronormativity that resists and

gradually, subversively, erodes not only the temporal binary opposition of 'past' and 'future,' but also the heteronormative binary of 'male' and 'female.'

In *The Unintentional Time Traveler* and *Orlando*, time travel naturalises the process of gender change, with the passage of time to the past and to the future transforming the protagonist into another gender and into another sex. In the short story 'All You Zombies,' the destabilisation of temporal continuity disrupts the protagonist's gender continuity, and aids in the reader's suspension of disbelief that such disruptions can occur.

All three narratives begin from the perspective of a seemingly heterosexual, cisgender male protagonist. The protagonist's gender identity is then deconstructed through time travel. Thus, the origin of each story is the heteronormative *status quo*, which then unwinds and expands outwards into less limited notions of gender. Essentially, the fictional trope of time travel exposes the 'more exuberantly sensual effects of temporal alterity and its vision of how temporal dislocation might produce new orientations of desire' (Freeman, 2010, p. 16), these new gender and sexual orientations being queer and deliberately non-heteronormative. In the primary texts, the 'temporal misalignments' of time travel 'can be the means of opening up other possible worlds' (Freeman, 2010, p. 16), specifically, queer worlds.

Social and Literary Context

Time travel is a long-established trope in speculative fiction. The distinctive subgenre of gender-change-through-time-travel has seen a marked growth since the advent of New Wave science fiction in the 1960s (Lacey, 2019, pp. 367-379), occurring alongside the sexual revolution and following the publication of the two Kinsey Reports in 1948 and 1953, which brought into mainstream discourse questions of sexuality and gender, and which 'challenged the idea of a fixed, knowable sexual orientation' (Lecklider, 2018, p. 206). This, in turn, inspired a more pronounced questioning of fixed sexual and gender identities in the science fiction and speculative fiction of the 1960s and beyond, through novels such as Theodore Sturgeon's *Venus Plus X* (1960), Brian Aldiss's *The Dark Light Years* (1964), Ursula K. Le Guin's *The Left Hand of Darkness* (1969), Isaac Asimov's *The Gods Themselves* (1972), and Marge Piercy's *Woman on the Edge of Time* (1976). 'I Remember Babylon,' a 1960 short story by Arthur C. Clarke, explicitly referenced the Kinsey Reports.

Most recently, the burgeoning preoccupation with gender politics in popular culture (Negra and Tasker, 2007, pp. 17-18), and 'the heightened popularity and visibility in popular culture' of 'non-binary gender identities and expressions' (McNabb, 2018, p. 55), has led to the resurgence of this subgenre. There is now a plethora of narratives that interrogate the notion of binary gender by interrogating the notion of binary time, although I have chosen the three primary texts for engaging more explicitly with this trope, and for it forming the core of each text's plot. Broader examples of the trope from roughly the last two decades include *This Is How You Lose the Time War* by Amal El-Mohtar and Max Gladstone (2019), *Glasshouse* by Charles Stross (2007), *Commitment Hour* by James Alan Gardner (1998), *Newton's Niece* by

Derek Beaven (1999), 'A Hollow Play' by Amal El-Mohtar (2013), 'The Night Train' by Lavie Tidhar (2010), and several stories from the anthologies, *Love Beyond Body, Space, and Time: An Indigenous LGBT Sci-Fi Anthology* (2016), and *Beyond Binary: Genderqueer and Sexually Fluid Speculative Fiction* (2012). There is an even greater prevalence of this trope in contemporary graphic novels and comic books, such as *Chronin: The Knife At Your Back* by Alison Wilgus (2019), and in movies and television series, such as the non-binary aliens of the *Stark Trek* franchise (McNabb, 2018, p. 55) and the newly female incarnation of the time-travelling Doctor Who (Cole, 2018), with 'the well-traveled heroic Time Lord supersed[ing] any binary demarcations of gender' (Powers, 2016, p. 205). In the above narratives, time travel is often used as a vehicle and metaphor for gender change, not only because of a wider interest in issues of gender identity and gender liberation overall, but because of a growing fascination with 'upending the convention that when it comes to gender and sexuality, there are only two options for each: male or female, gay or straight,' especially 'as an increasing number of people say they aren't one or the other but perhaps neither or maybe both' (Steinmetz, 2017).

Despite the expanding popularity of time travel being used as a literary device to deconstruct binary gender, there is a dearth of research into this trope. The closest study that I found to mine is 'The Queer Body as Time Machine' by Tara East (2018), but only one of the primary texts used in East's paper overlaps with my book, and East's paper engages exclusively with FTM (female-to-male) transitions. There is a need for more scholarly engagement with this trope, because there are now enough works of speculative fiction exploring gender through time travel that it has become an identifiable subgenre of its own. My book addresses this need.

Methodology

I explore this trope within my three chosen primary texts by employing a mixed methodology of intersectionality that combines gender studies, queer theory and literary theory. As I will explain below, I combine the insights of key scholars including Mikhail Bakhtin, Jacques Derrida, Judith Butler, Jack Halberstam, José Esteban Muñoz, Annamarie Jagose and Eve Kosofsky Sedgwick to produce an interdisciplinary reading of the primary texts that synthesises gender and time. However, in order to explain my approach further, I must first define some key terms.

Key Terms

This section contains definitions of the main terms that will be used recurrently within the book, although those terms will, of course, be unpacked in deeper, text-specific detail in each chapter. The key terms are **queer**, **queer time**, **chronotope**, **deconstruction** and **gender performance**.

While 'queer' is a blanket term generally referring to LGBTQIA+ people and issues, queer theorist Annamarie Jagose observes that the term has a problematic history from which it has recently been reclaimed, and that it is still undergoing revisions:

> Once the term 'queer' was, at best, slang for homosexual, at worst, a term of homophobic abuse. In recent years

'queer' has come to be used differently, sometimes as an umbrella term for a coalition of culturally marginal sexual self-identifications and at other times to describe a nascent theoretical model which has developed out of more traditional lesbian and gay studies. What is clear... is that queer is very much a category in the process of formation. It is not simply that queer has yet to solidify and take on a more consistent profile, but rather that its definitional indeterminacy, its elasticity, is one of its constituent characteristics.' (Jagose, 1996, p. 1)

The very 'elasticity' of the term 'queer' allows for a deeper engagement with the often amorphous complexities of sexuality and gender identity than would be possible within the constraints of any one definition, and allows the term to be open to potentialities that may not yet have been explored, in what Muñoz calls a 'queer futurity' (2009, p. 185). If 'queerness is not yet here but it approaches like a crashing wave of potentiality' (Muñoz, 2009, p. 185), then the term 'queer' is perpetually arriving, never arrived; the word is never definitionally finite, closed or conclusive, but all the more powerful and inclusive for it. As Jagose says above, 'queer' is an organic term that has evolved alongside the changing social mores and conventions of our times and of the LGBTQIA+ movement. In reference to literature, the term 'queer' can be defined thus:

Art is fiction that is beautiful, appealing, of more than ordinary substance and cultural longevity. It speaks to us across time. If we assume that good fiction deconstructs cultural cliché by writing about individual, particular characters in individual, particular situations, and if we define as queer any fiction which destabilises the assumptions that underpin the construction of sexual identity, then all really good fiction whose particulars include reference to sex and gender can't be anything other than queer. War machine and time machine. (Eskridge and Griffith, 2008, p. 48)

This definition, while broad, fits each of the primary texts I have selected. They do speak to us 'across time' and through the narratological 'time machine' of time travel, which is simultaneously a 'war machine' waging war on heteronormativity. Indeed, the protagonists of all three primary texts—Orlando from *Orlando*, the Bartender from 'All You Zombies' and Jack/Jacqueline from *The Unintentional Time Traveler*—confound limited, binary notions of gender, and frequently occupy liminal spaces between genders or contain memories of multiple genders at once. The term 'queer' is thus appropriate to use when referring to these texts and to their main characters, who often defy neat, easy-to-define labels. The protagonist of 'All You Zombies,' for example, is explicitly defined as intersex only during one time-state, but in other time-states identifies as a man or a woman.

Consequently, the principle of 'queer time' is also important to this book, as it informs many of my analyses in subsequent chapters. The tyranny of heteronormativity, Halberstam argues, is inseparable from the tyranny of the gender binary, because that binary forms the basis of heteronormativity in the first place. In order to counteract these dual, interlinked tyrannies, Halberstam proposes a queer view of time, or a 'queer time,' which is 'a term for those specific models of temporality that emerge... once one leaves the temporal frames of... reproduction and family, longevity, risk/safety, and inheritance' (2005, p. 6). 'Straight time,' conversely, is 'discretely divisible' and 'linear' (Muñoz, 2009, p. 154), and reinforces the hegemonic binary structures of time (past/future) and gender (male/female). The concept of 'queer time' can be a 'queer lens' (Edwards, 2009, p. 59) through which to read the primary texts, since all the protagonists are queer as regards to their gender and/or sexual identity. Each of the primary texts engages with queer time by disrupting or dismantling straight time, either through non-linear time travel between time-states, or through the metaphorical deconstruction of linear, binary time and linear, binary gender.

Next, I will define the term 'chronotope.' Bakhtin, a leading scholar in the field of narratology, invented a term known as the 'chronotope' (Bakhtin, 1981, p. 84), which literally translates into 'time-space' and is defined as the means by which time and space are expressed in narrative. This is directly relevant to my book, as time travel in itself is a temporal narrative construct. In the three primary texts I study, the temporal aspect of the chronotope is the transportation through time of the protagonist, while the spatial aspect of the chronotope is the physical and psychological space of the gendered body. As Aristotle says, 'it is by means of the body that is carried along that we become aware of the before and after in the motion, and if we regard these as countable we get the "now" ' (1984, p. 372)[1]. *All* bodies are chronotopes in that they allow us to travel through time, to 'become aware of the before and

---

1. This quote is from Aristotle's *Physics*, 219b24-25. The reference provided is for the book containing the quote.

after.' In that sense, we are all time travellers, just as the protagonists of the primary texts are; what distinguishes them from us, however, is that their time-travelling is textual, and is specifically intended to deconstruct gender. Thus, the chronotope in these stories is the gendered body that travels through time.

Now, we come to the term 'deconstruction,' which seems at first to resist definition because, as Derrida says, 'All sentences of the type 'deconstruction is X' or 'deconstruction is not X' *a priori* miss the point' (qtd. in Norris, 1987, pp. 19-20). Nonetheless, a definition must be attempted if one is to use the term in productive discourse. In a queer, feminist reading, deconstruction can aid in the reclamation of that which was lost, oppressed or erased, such as speech, agency or textual representation. If 'meanings are… constructed through dichotomies or binary oppositions,' such as the male/female binary opposition of gender, and such an opposition always privileges, or 'makes present,' one half of the opposition above the other, which is made 'absent,' then 'the aim of deconstruction is to problematise the present term and to reclaim the absent one' (Mumby and Putnam, 2001, p. 1247). And yet, deconstruction does not aim to 'reverse binary oppositions but to problematise the very idea of opposition and the notion of identity upon which it depends' (Poovey, 1988, p. 52). The primary texts examined in this book do not simply reverse the heteronormative, male/female binary opposition of gender, but problematise *the entire system of interrelated oppositions* that constructs heteronormativity, such as masculine/feminine, heterosexual/homosexual, normal/abnormal, cisgender/transgender, et cetera, and question whether identity must always be predicated on the opposition between self and other, or whether there may be a more inclusive, less oppositional approach. Norris explains that deconstruction is 'seizing on precisely those unregarded details... which are always, and necessarily, passed over by interpreters of a more orthodox persuasion' (1987, p. 19). Heteronormativity is the orthodox persuasion whose unregarded details the primary texts seize upon and deconstruct, so that they may propose other ways of seeing and being.

Deconstruction is not, despite its name, destructive, nor does it seek to outright destroy an 'existing structure' like the heteronormative gender binary; rather, it is more of a systematic dismantling, and 'such a dismantling of a structure may reveal something new about that building itself which was previously concealed' (Michener, 2016, p. 64). The primary texts studied in this book dismantle time and gender in this manner. By portraying time as non-linear and non-binary, they explore what may lie beneath the surface of our mundane, everyday understanding of time as linear, monodirectional and as that which passes; similarly, in dismantling the gender binary, they explore what lies beneath the illusory binary opposition of male and female, and if 'something new,' or something lost, oppressed, or erased, can be revealed about gender identity when the binary strictures of straight time are deconstructed. Deconstruction consists of the 'overturning and displacing [of] a conceptual order, as well as the nonconceptual order with which the conceptual order is articulated' (Derrida, 1982, p. 329), meaning, in the context of this book, that the primary texts overturn and displace the conceptual order of binary gender, as well as the nonconceptual order that is the spontaneous, experiential consciousness of the body itself, the gender performativity of which is how that conceptual order is generally articulated.

This brings us to the issue of gender performance, or the 'gendered stylisation of the body' (Butler, 2010, p. xv) through clothing, mannerisms and other social cues. Butler asserts that the body 'becomes its gender through a series of acts which are renewed, revised, and consolidated through time' (1988, p. 523). This view of gender as a performative and inherently metamorphosal process, and hence as a temporal phenomenon, is central to the investigation of the chronotope in this work. Butler asserts that 'performativity is not a singular act, but a repetition and a ritual, which achieves its effects through its naturalisation in the context of a body, understood, in part, as a culturally sustained temporal duration' (Butler, 2010, p. xv). Time travel is used in each of the primary texts to naturalise not only the process of sex and gender change within the protagonists, but also the changes in their outward gender performativity. This culminates in a deconstruction of gender that is accomplished by disrupting the flow of the 'sustained temporal duration' of any one gender or body. Butler defines gender as performativity by an agent, rather than as a presumed innate, *a priori* construct that is predetermined and that cannot be influenced by time or action. According to Butler, the epistemological definition of gender is *a posteriori*, not *a priori* (Baehr, 2006), and thus leaves room for queer revisionings, performances and reinterpretations of gender, instead of constantly privileging the *a priori* dominance of a heteronormative gender binary.

My argument is that in all three stories, the queer chronotope of the time-travelling gendered body enables the protagonists' gender identity to be 'renewed, revised and consolidated through time,' which in turn aids in the deconstruction of the male/female binary towards a non-binary, non-linear temporality of gender.

Chapters

The book contains three main chapters, each addressing one of the primary texts and exploring how that text deconstructs the gender binary through time travel.

Chapter One studies how the novel *Orlando* by Virginia Woolf deconstructs the male/female gender binary by deconstructing the past/future time binary. The protagonist's sex change challenges the linearity of 'straight time,' in which the causality of gender is monodirectional, queer agency is impossible, and a false equivalency is drawn between gender identity and biological sex. The text instead leads Orlando (and the reader) away from straight time and into queer time, which is multidirectional, non-linear and non-heteronormative, and which unhitches gender identity at least partially from biological sex through a process that I call 'gender lag.' This lag grants queer agency to Orlando in terms of his/her own gender identity and gender performativity. In exercising queer agency, Orlando's changing body becomes a queer 'chronotope,' that is, a queer expression of time and space within the narrative. Explored in the chapter are the various means employed within the text to queer time and gender. The cultural context within which *Orlando* was written is also considered as a contributing factor to the subtextuality of its queerness. Finally, the text's transgender connotations are analysed.

Chapter Two studies how Robert A. Heinlein's 'All You Zombies,' a time travel story, uses the disruption of temporal continuity to disrupt heteronormativity. The chapter combines queer theory, gender studies and narratology to analyse the interplay between time and gender within the story, and how that interplay allows the textual revisioning and rediscovery of the initially heterosexual, cisgender-seeming protagonist as a queer person. The time-travelling intersex protagonist personifies the deconstruction of gender, and embodies the constant negotiation between determinism and agency that defines gender identity and sexuality. I will explore how the story's protagonist, who identifies as male or female at different times and who becomes his/her own mother *and* father through time travel, queers reproduction through a non-linear time loop, revisions queer desire as a desire for the self, and dismantles binary gender through the subversion of the masculine language register usually used in detective noir fiction.

Chapter Three focuses on *The Unintentional Time Traveler* by Everett Maroon. Maroon's novel is an example of how contemporary speculative fiction engages with social issues such as gender. In the case of this novel, time travel is the catalyst for providing social commentary on standard, heteronormative notions of gender. *The Unintentional Time Traveler* explores issues of gender identity through the sex-changing protagonist, Jack, who travels back in time to Prohibition-era America and becomes a girl named Jacqueline. The tension between Jack's and Jacqueline's sexes and genders is used to unpack the social and psychological implications of being transgender. The novel deconstructs the male/female gender binary through the textual process of 'transing time,' while also taking a reparative approach to resisting the pathologisation of transness and the system of heteronormative, cisgender privilege that supports it. I will unpack how the text's transgender themes interrogate the gender binary, and how these themes are a form of both reparative reading and reparative writing, instead of the 'paranoid reading' (Sedgwick, 2003, p. 126) that results in the false pathologisation of transgender individuals.

The analyses of all three chapters will then be drawn together in the conclusion, which will make a final statement about what the subgenre of gender-change-through-time-travel accomplishes, and what possibilities for queering gender it may hold as it continues to be popularised.

References

Aldiss, B. (1964) *The Dark Light Years*. New York: Signet Books.

Aristotle. (1984) *Complete Works of Aristotle, Volume 1: The Revised Oxford Translation*. Edited by Jonathan Barnes. Princeton: Princeton University Press.

Asimov, I. (1972) *The Gods Themselves*. New York: Doubleday.

Baehr, J.S. (2006) 'A Priori and A Posteriori,' *Internet Encyclopedia of Philosophy* [online]. Available at: <https://www.iep.utm.edu/apriori/> (Accessed: 25 February 2020).

Bakhtin, M. (1981) *The Dialogic Imagination*. Austin: Texas University Press.

Beaven, D. (1999) *Newton's Niece*. London: Fourth Estate.

Butler, J. (2010) *Gender Trouble: Feminism and the Subversion of Identity*. New York: Routledge.
---. (1988) 'Performative Acts and Gender Constitution: An Essay in Phenomenology and Feminist Theory,' *Theatre Journal*, 40(4), pp. 519–531.

Clarke, A.C. (1960) 'I Remember Babylon,' *Playboy*, 7(5), May, pp. 94-100.

Cole, S. (2018) *Doctor Who: Combat Magicks*. London: BBC Books.

Derrida, J. (1982) *Margins of Philosophy*. Translated by A. Bass. Chicago: Chicago University Press.
---. (1973) *Speech and Phenomena: And Other essays on Husserl's Theory of Signs*. Translated by D. Allison. Evanston: Northwestern University Press.

East, T. (2018) 'The Queer Body as Time Machine,' *Writing From Below*, 4(1) [online]. Available at: <https://writingfrombelow.org/science-fiction/the-queer-body-as-time-machine/> (Accessed 25 February 2020).

Edwards, J. (2009) *Eve Kosofsky Sedgwick*. New York: Routledge.

El-Mohtar, A. (2013) 'A Hollow Play.' *Apex Book Company* [online]. Available at: <https://www.apexbookcompany.com/blogs/frontpage/15748153-a-hollow-play-by-amal-el-mohtar> (Accessed 25 February 2020).
---. and Gladstone, M. (2019) *This Is How You Lose the Time War*. New York: Saga Press.

Eskridge, K. and Griffith, N. (2008) 'War Machine, Time Machine' in Pearson, W.G., Gordon, J. and Hollinger, V. (eds.) *Queer Universes: Sexualities in Science Fiction*. Liverpool: Liverpool University Press, pp. 39-51.

Freeman, E. (2010) *Time Binds: Queer Temporalities, Queer Histories*. Durham: Duke University Press.

Gardner, J.A. (1998) *Commitment Hour*. New York: Avon Eos.

Halberstam, J. (2005) *In a Queer Time and Space*. New York: New York University Press.

Heinlein, R.A. (2013) '—All You Zombies—.' Spectrum Literary Agency.

Jagose, A. (1996) *Queer Theory: An Introduction*. Melbourne: Melbourne University Press.

Lacey, L.J. (2019) 'Science Fiction, Gender, and Sexuality in the New Wave' in Canavan, G. and Link, E.C. (eds.) *The Cambridge History of Science Fiction*. Cambridge: Cambridge University Press, pp. 367-379.

Le Guin, U.K. (1969) *The Left Hand of Darkness*. New York: Ace Books.

Lecklider, A. (2018) 'Public Excursions in Fierce Truth-Telling: Literary Cultures and Homosexuality' in Vials, C. (ed.) *American Literature in Transition*, 1940–1950. Cambridge: Cambridge University Press, pp. 193-211.

Mandelo, B. (2012) *Beyond Binary: Genderqueer and Sexually Fluid Speculative Fiction*. New Jersey: Lethe Press.

Maroon, E. (2016) *The Unintentional Time Traveler*. New Jersey: Lethe Press.

McNabb, C. (2018) *Nonbinary Gender Identities: History, Culture, Resources*. Lanham: Rowman & Littlefield.

Michener, R.T. (2016) *Engaging Deconstructive Theology*. New York: Routledge.

Mumby, D.K. and Putnam, L.L. (2001) 'The Politics of Emotion: A feminist reading of bounded rationality' in *Organizational Studies Volume III: Selves and Subjects*. New York: Routledge.

Muñoz, J.E. (2009) *Cruising Utopia: The Then and There of Queer Futurity*. New York: New York University Press.

Negra, D. and Tasker, Y. (eds.) (2007) *Interrogating Postfeminism: Gender and the Politics of Popular Culture*. Durham: Duke University Press.

Nicholson, H. (ed.) (2016) *Love Beyond Body, Space, and Time: An Indigenous LGBT Sci-Fi Anthology*. Winnipeg: Bedside Press.

Norris, C. (1987) *Derrida*. London: Fontana Press.

Piercy, M. (1976) *Woman on the Edge of Time*. New York: Alfred A. Knopf.

Poovey, M. (1988) 'Feminism and Deconstruction,' *Feminist Studies*, 14(1), pp. 51-65.

Powers, T. (2016) *Gender and the Quest in British Science Fiction Television: An Analysis of Doctor Who, Blake's 7, Red Dwarf and Torchwood*. Jefferson: McFarland & Company.

Sedgwick, E.K. (2003) *Touching Feeling: Affect, Pedagogy, Performativity*. Durham: Duke University Press.

Steinmetz, K. (2017) 'Beyond "He" or "She": The Changing Meaning of Gender and Sexuality,' *TIME Magazine*, 16 March [online]. Available at: <https://time.com/magazine/us/4703292/march-27th-2017-vol-189-no-11-u-s/> (Accessed on: 25 February 2020).

Stross, C. (2007) *Glasshouse*. New York: Ace Books.

Sturgeon, T. (1960) *Venus Plus X*. Salem: Pyramid Books.

Tidhar, L. (2010) 'The Night Train,' *Strange Horizons*, 14 June [online]. Available at: <http://strangehorizons.com/fiction/the-night-train/> (Accessed 25 February 2020).

Wilgus, A. (2019) *Chronin: The Knife At Your Back*. New York: Tor.

Woolf, V. (2015) *Orlando: A Biography*. EBooks@Adelaide [online]. Available at: <https://ebooks.adelaide.edu.au/w/woolf/virginia/w91o/complete.html> (Accessed 26 October 2019).

CHAPTER ONE

The Temporal Body as Queer Chronotope in Virginia Woolf's *Orlando*

[Q]ueerness is not yet here but it approaches like a
crashing wave of potentiality.
— José Esteban Muñoz, *Cruising Utopia*.

Introduction

The titular protagonist of *Orlando* changes sex and gender,
and in so doing disrupts and subverts linear, binary time.
In this chapter, I will explore how this subversion queers
time within the narrative. I will analyse the text through
Eve Kosofsky Sedgwick's 'queer lens' (Edwards, 2009, p.
59), not only because 'Virginia Woolf's affair with Vita
Sackville-West, to whom she dedicated *Orlando*, is a clear
indication that the novel necessitates a queer reading'
(Paludi, 2012, p. 184), but because such a reading is
required to decode the queer subtext underlying Woolf's
characterisation of Orlando. The phrase 'queer reading'
is often shortened to 'queering' and can describe the
proactive engagement with, and textual interpretation of,
'the open mesh of possibilities, gaps, overlaps, dissonances
and resonances, lapses and excesses of meaning when
the constituent elements of anyone's gender, of anyone's

sexuality aren't made (or *can't be* made) to signify monolithically' (Sedgwick, 2013, p. 8).

Orlando's gender and sexuality do not signify monolithically, either temporally or spatially. I will use the methodology of queering to argue that Orlando's body-across-time, or temporal body, is what Mikhail Bakhtin calls a 'chronotope' (Bakhtin, 1981, p. 84), a term that translates into 'time-space' and defines how time and space are expressed in narrative. In *Orlando*, the temporal aspect of the chronotope is the protagonist's journey through time, while its spatial aspect is the physical and psychological space of the protagonist's body, which extends to and includes the body's gender. Orlando's sex and gender transition makes Orlando's body a living 'time-space,' a gendered and gender-altering space that travels across time and has its own non-linear, non-binary, non-heteronormative chronology.

In essence, Orlando's body is a chronotope because it 'is not a 'body' at all but a figure for relations between bodies past and present' (Freeman, 2010, p. 116), i.e. between Orlando's male (past) and female (present) bodies. This also makes it a queer chronotope, because Orlando's embodiment of multiple gendered states results in Orlando possessing a genderfluid psychology that is inherently queer. The sex/gender change that is central to the novel's plot disrupts and deconstructs the discretely divisible, linear conventions of straight time, which is defined by queer theorist José Esteban Muñoz as 'not just […] a bias related to sexual object choice but […] [a] dominant and overarching temporal and spatial organisation of the world' (Muñoz, 2009, p. 154). Orlando's spatiotemporal transformation reorganises a worldview built on the heteronormative, male/female gender binary, and contains 'the potential to help us encounter a queer temporality [...] a thing that is not linearity' (Muñoz, 2009, p. 186).

As a queer chronotope, Orlando's changing body challenges the notion of binary gender, i.e. the binary opposition of male/female, by challenging the notion of binary time, that is, the binary opposition of past/future. It is this deconstruction of gender and time, through the subtextual queering of time and body, that the chapter studies.

Cultural Context

Before launching into an analysis of the text itself, I must provide the necessary cultural context that explains why *Orlando*'s queerness is more subtextual than textual, and why the text's approach to heteronormativity is more subversive than openly confrontational. The queer subtext of the novel lies in its use of ellipsis, wherein frank discussions of sexuality and gender identity exist in a fade-to-black liminality between the text and its queer shadow: 'But let other pens treat of sex and sexuality; we quit such odious subjects as soon as we can' (*Orlando*, ch. 3, par. 43)[1]. In so saying, the narrator directly addresses the reader (and, specifically, the censor), slyly implying that the omission of these so-called 'odious' matters is deliberate but not entirely voluntary, especially considering Woolf's own resistance to the censorship of her era, as discussed below.

Due to the social, sexual and literary conservatism of Woolf's time, the non-heteronormativity of *Orlando*

---

1. Any further in-text citations of *Orlando* will follow this format.

remains largely subtextual, and is necessarily couched in the language of the very heteronormativity it seeks to unravel. Subversion can only occur within the system; once one is outside a system, only rebellion is possible, and that is a far less subtle—and sometimes far less effective—mode of resistance. Subversion must borrow the language of the system, must use its letters to spell out new words, new meanings, in a code truly visible and understandable only to fellow saboteurs of the *status quo*, who, through their seeming conformity, go unremarked upon by that *status quo* until many of its central tenets have already been partly deconstructed and reclaimed. This is a phenomenon deeply familiar to the LGBTQIA+ community, in which the slow, painstaking dismantling of heteronormativity has often involved using 'a coded lexicon' (Smorag, 2008, p. 2) to escape persecution, while also reclaiming language originally used by a heteronormative society to oppress the community, such as the words 'queer' and 'gay' (Smorag, 2008, p. 5). Orlando's reclamation of the words 'woman' and 'man' from the gender binary is similarly coded in a subtle and ultimately subversive queer code.

The sexual mores of Woolf's time certainly dictated subtlety as a matter of course, and are hinted at in Orlando's somewhat mocking description of nineteenth-century modesty, which nonetheless was not much more immodest in the early twentieth century, when *Orlando* was written: 'Love, birth, and death were all swaddled in a variety of fine phrases […] Evasions and concealments were sedulously practised' (*Orlando*, ch. 5, par. 3). Thus, the novel's themes of queerness and gender non-conformity are covertly explored through '[e]vasions and concealments,' such as the magical realism of Orlando's transformation-through-sleep, which is a narratological abstraction that disingenuously invites the reader to suspend their disbelief regarding the abruptness of Orlando's sex change.

This textual coyness in openly expressing non-heteronormativity is partly Orlando's, as a character whose roots lie three hundred years in the past—a far more conservative past—and partly the text's. It is an understated, undercover resistance to the prevailing hegemonic narrative of the gender binary as it reigned in the early twentieth century. A post-transition Orlando comments that the experience of womanhood is 'to resist and to yield; to yield and to resist' (*Orlando*, ch. 4, par. 5). Forced into indirect means of resistance—including passive or manipulative resistance—by the patriarchy, the women of Orlando's world, be it in *his* past or *her* present, are depicted as finding the stretching of the resisting/yielding dichotomy as the only real power afforded to them. This is a means of resistance also familiar to the queer community at the time when *Orlando* was written. It was in the 1920s that 'the semantic shift from « unusual » to « unusual sexual orientation »' first occurred (Smorag, 2008, p. 5), and it was in 1921, a mere seven years before *Orlando*'s publication, that Britain's *Criminal Law Amendment Act* attempted to make sexual acts of 'gross indecency between females' illegal (Derry, 2018, p. 245). While the amendment never became law, the fact that it passed the House of Commons and almost *did* become law was nevertheless a threat hanging over queer women such as Woolf.

Hence *Orlando*'s (the text's) coyness, which contradicts, in most instances, Orlando's (the character's) frankness.

Here, too, the resisting/yielding dichotomy is embodied and then deconstructed *within the text itself,* narrator and narrative seemingly (and fruitfully) at odds. As one sexual historian says of the decades surrounding and immediately following *Orlando*'s creation, and specifically of the year 1949 in which the infamous 'Little Kinsey' report was first compiled, the gap between how sexuality was expressed and how it was hidden could be explained by drawing 'a temporal (and gendered) distance, and say that the time had not yet arrived when such statements could be 'heard' and understood' (Stanley, 2014, p. 217). This was not very different from the social milieu surrounding *Orlando*'s publication in 1928, twenty-one years prior to the compilation of the 'Little Kinsey' report, and, as stated in the previous paragraph, seven years after the attempted outlawing of lesbian sex in England. The question remains whether *Orlando*'s queerness is subtextual primarily because it could not be 'heard and understood' by the society of Woolf's time, or because that subtextuality rendered the protagonist's queerness open-ended and ripe for interpretation as several sorts of queerness, be it transgenderism, bigenderism, agenderism, bisexuality, homosexuality, or something else. In not textually specifying or labelling Orlando's gender identity and sexual orientation, the novel becomes a fertile ground for open-ended potentialities of queerness, while at the same time remaining bound by the chains of heteronormativity that are never explicitly shattered and, as a result, are never wholly overcome. This peculiar admixture of liberation and oppression is yet another example of the resisting/yielding dynamic and is precisely what Orlando experiences in the transition between genders, going from a permissive existence as a man to a restrictive one as a woman, wherein women are not even granted the right to an education: 'Ignorant and poor as we [women] are compared with the other sex [...] armoured with every weapon as they are [...] they debar us even from a knowledge of the alphabet' (*Orlando*, ch. 4, par. 10).

The text seems to disdain outright expressions of queerness. When Archduke Harry confesses that, despite being a man, he had longed for Orlando's earlier male self and had gone so far as to cross-dress as a woman in order to win him, it is a revelation that is treated with disgust and contempt by Orlando, who says, 'If this is love [...] there is something highly ridiculous about it' (*Orlando*, ch. 4, par. 36). While it may not be Harry's bisexuality that Orlando is condemning, but rather the degree to which Harry sacrificed his dignity for love, it is nonetheless a bracing reminder that, at least in Orlando's era, queerness must be subtextual and kept to the margins, or risk being ridiculed (if not legally punished).

Orlando's simultaneous conformity and resistance to heteronormative standards, as well as Orlando's self-conscious criticisms of the patriarchy and of his/her own occasional obedience to it, 'brings feminism squarely into the queer realm by confronting the sexually ambiguous protagonist with his/her own complicity in the misogynist sex/gender system' (Hankins, 1997, p. 182). Orlando is in the process of perpetual escape from this system, but it is nevertheless a system that Orlando is sometimes forced to occupy. As Freeman says, '*Orlando* retrospectively looks back [...] to discredited historiographic methods and restores an eroticised materiality to the gaps and imperfect sutures between past and present' (Freeman, 2010, p. 111). In this sense, Orlando's body is a queer chronotope incarnate that draws 'a temporal (and gendered) distance' (Stanley, 2014, p. 105) between past and present, male and female, straight and suggestively non-straight (if not outright queer). My queer reading of *Orlando* allows me to 'take in the queerness that is embedded in the gesture' (Muñoz, 2009, p. 72) of Woolf's dedication of the novel to her lover, Vita Sackville-West, and of Woolf's deliberate authorial choice of changing the protagonist's sex and gender partway through the novel.

Another revealing choice is Woolf's deployment of the word 'queer' itself. It makes an appearance relatively early in the novel, when the narrator professes to being conscious of time's relativity and of the contrast between internal versus external time:

> But Time, unfortunately, though it makes animals and vegetables bloom and fade with amazing punctuality, has no such simple effect upon the mind of man. The mind of man, moreover, works with equal strangeness upon the body of time. An hour, once it lodges in the queer element of the human spirit, may be stretched to fifty or a hundred times its clock length; on the other hand, an hour may be accurately represented on the timepiece of the mind by one second. This extraordinary discrepancy between time on the clock and time in the mind is less known than it should be and deserves fuller investigation. (*Orlando*, ch. 2, par. 37)

The novel itself conducts such an investigation through the queer chronotope of Orlando's body, which is an incarnation of 'the body of time' as it is lodged in 'the queer element of the human spirit.' Now, the use of the term 'queer' in the above excerpt may or may not refer to queerness as an umbrella term for non-heteronormative gender identities and sexualities, but it is worth noting that by 1928, when *Orlando* was written, the word 'queer' had already taken on a connotation of sexual and gender non-conformity, although the word was largely pejorative then and had not yet been publicly reclaimed by the LGBTQIA+ community, as it has been today. Elspeth H. Brown, a queer historian, notes that 'queer' is 'a historical term that emerged in the early twentieth century to connote homosexuality as a specific expression of the term's older meaning as odd, bent, or peculiar' (Brown, 2019, p. 9). Woolf's own involvement in the queer literary community via Bloomsbury, a 'chosen community' of queer writers such as E. M. Forster and Lytton Strachey, was based on 'the sharing of unsanctioned and unconventional sexual preferences, especially homosexual preferences' (Vanita, 1997, p. 165). This indicates that Woolf would likely have known the non-heteronormative connotations of the word 'queer,' and if so, was noting, in the above passage, the discrepancy between external straight time, which maps with 'amazing punctuality' such socially accepted chronologies as the heterosexual reproduction of animals, and internal queer time, which telescopes or collapses time into more relative, non-binary notions of belonging and identity.

However, given the legal ramifications of the censorship laws in 1928 that threatened court trials for authors who explored queerness in their texts, Woolf had to play 'an elaborate game of hide and seek with the reader and the censor' (Hankins, 1997, p. 181). She had to couch the queerness of the novel in the sex-changing chronotope of Orlando's body, a conceptual 'Trojan horse' intended to smuggle queer 'contraband' (Hankins, 1997, p. 187) past the eye of the censor. Woolf engaged with the censorship of LGBTQIA+ content both as an author and as a 'political activist' who attempted to 'testify in the Hall trial' (Hankins, 1997, p. 183), that is, in the censorship trial of Radclyffe Hall's lesbian novel *The Well of Loneliness* (1928). Woolf's lover, Vita Sackville-West, also had a run-in with the authorities in 1924 regarding West's novel *Challenge* (1974). West was forced to change the sex of a lesbian character in order to 'provide the required heterosexual couple' (Hankins, 1997, p. 183). That Woolf then went on to deliberately use a sex change as the central plot point of her own novel is a sign that Woolf 'chose to laugh at the censor' (Hankins, 1997, p. 183) while still conducting a subversion of heteronormativity through the subtextual queerness of *Orlando*, as studied below.

The Universal Non-Binary

Throughout the novel, Orlando's gender performance is a negotiation between the self and the external world, and is an expression of an inner genderfluidity that, the text postulates, may very well be shared by *all* people to varying degrees, even by those who consciously subscribe to the gender binary. Despite the seeming fantasticality of Orlando's transformation, the narrator of the novel makes it clear that Orlando's genderfluidity is not supernatural but in fact very natural, and is symbolic of a universal human experience:

[P]erhaps in this she was only expressing rather more openly than usual […] something that happens to most people without being thus plainly expressed. […] Different though the sexes are, they intermix. In every human being a vacillation from one sex to the other takes place, and often it is only the clothes that keep the male or female likeness, while underneath the sex is the very opposite of what it is above. Of the complications and confusions which thus result everyone has had experience; but here we leave the general question and note only the odd effect it had in the particular case of Orlando herself. […] For it was this mixture in her of man and woman, one being uppermost and then the other, that often gave her conduct an unexpected turn. […] Whether, then, Orlando was most man or woman, it is difficult to say and cannot now be decided. (*Orlando*, ch. 4, pars. 51-52)

Orlando's transformation is only the making visible of the 'complications and confusions' that arise from the embodiment and expression of a universal non-binary gender identity in a binary world, a world that seeks to divide people into two neat, gendered categories, even though those people may defy such a categorisation within themselves.

Categorisation and narrativisation are inextricably linked and contribute to each other; the categorisation built into the gender binary generates a narrative of heterosexual primacy and preponderance. Annamarie Jagose argues that the temporal sequencing born of narrativisation regulates and normalises heteronormativity, and that the narrative of heteronormativity itself feeds back into the categorisation of the gender binary:

Purporting to do nothing more than take instruction from
the principles of temporal order, sequence underwrites
those regulatory narratives that establish heterosexuality
as the most developed form of sexual identification and
homosexuality as a not-quite heterosexual disposition […]
In this charged context, sequence—what comes before
and what comes after—often tips into precedence—what
comes first and what comes second […] [T]he cultural
insistence on the sequential nature of sexuality—its
preconditions and final outcomes, its causally connected
development—defends less against homosexuality per
se than against an undifferentiated sexual desire—the
polymorphous drives and impulses of which exceed easy
narrativisation. (Jagose, 2002, p. 101)

Orlando is a queer text because it determinedly
resists the 'easy narrativisation' of the gender binary by
portraying the 'polymorphous drives' of a protagonist
who is masculine *and* feminine, and who loves men *and*
women, while morphing in and out of male and female
bodies. Additionally, Orlando's abrupt, unexplained
transformation de-sequences the male/female gender
binary by disordering the social privileging of the male
half of the binary above the female half. The text does so
by demonstrating the essential humanness of each sex and
the continuity of Orlando's psychological identity through
both sexes. Orlando is Orlando regardless of being in a
man's body or a woman's; Orlando is, for example, a poet
and an inveterate romantic in both sexes. In fact, Orlando
continues writing the very same poem as a woman that
'he' had begun as a man:

Then Orlando felt in the bosom of her shirt as if for some locket or relic of lost affection, and drew out […] a roll of paper, sea-stained, blood-stained, travel-stained — the manuscript of her poem, 'The Oak Tree.' […] She turned back to the first page and read the date, 1586, written in her own boyish hand. She had been working at it for close three hundred years now. […] Yet through all these changes she had remained, she reflected, fundamentally the same. She had the same brooding meditative temper, the same love of animals and nature, the same passion for the country and the seasons. (*Orlando*, ch. 5, par. 13)

Orlando's internal continuity de-sequences the gender binary by creating a tautology between male and female, man and woman; regardless of sex, Orlando's selfhood and personhood remain the same, just as they remain the same regardless of the passage of time. Orlando's transformation resists the linear narrativisation of sexuality, sexual politics, gender identity and time. As Jagose explains above, temporal sequencing 'underwrites' the 'regulatory narratives' of heteronormativity that privilege heterosexual and cisgender identities. In *Orlando*, the de-sequencing of time and the deconstruction of the heteronormative gender binary are interconnected.

The past/future temporal binary can only exist in linear, sequential time. Woolf disdained the monodirectional linearity of realist fiction by referring to it as 'this appalling narrative business of the realist: getting on from lunch to dinner,' and claimed to be 'bored by narrative' (Woolf, 2003, p. 136, 138). By her own admission, Woolf much preferred to escape from 'the formal railway line of a sentence,' the linear plodding from narrative point A to narrative point B, because, as Woolf said, 'people don't and never did feel or think or dream for a second that way; but all over the place' (Woolf, qtd. in Bell, 1972, pp. 106-107). It is therefore not surprising that *Orlando* often escapes or dissolves the bounds of linear determinism in a fluid narrative that persistently resists being restricted to the time binary or the gender binary. Woolf scholar Elizabeth Abel argues that Woolf had a creative impetus 'to evade the tyranny of sequence by reshaping time as depth' (Abel, 1989, p. xvi). The 'reshaping' or spatialising of time taking place within Orlando's body defies the tyranny of sequence by de-sequencing its own sexual determinism, and by giving Orlando the added 'depth' of genderfluidity. The novel exists outside of straight time because it resists the linear, binary narrativisation of time and gender.

Straight Time to Queer Time

Muñoz asserts that '[q]ueerness's time is a stepping out of the linearity of straight time. Straight time is a self-naturalising temporality. Straight time's 'presentness' needs to be phenomenologically questioned' (Muñoz, 2009, p. 25). Orlando as a queer chronotope is a phenomenological questioning of straight time, and a journey out of straight time towards queer time.

The most transparent questioning of heteronormativity within the text is Orlando's sex/gender change, an event that 'that shoves one off course, out of straight time' (Muñoz, 2009, p. 155). Indeed, it shoves both Orlando and the reader out of straight time, because Orlando's transformation is 'a stepping out of time and place, leaving the here and now of straight time for a then and there that might be queer futurity' (Muñoz, 2009, p. 185). Orlando's subtextual queerness, existing in potentiality—in futurity—looms as large in the text as the Derridean myth of the origin (Lewis, 2008, p. 100), for even though Orlando's queerness is a futurity, it is also, definitionally, the source, since queer time is circular, recursive, non-linear and non-binary. Orlando does not suddenly become genderqueer; s/he was always genderqueer. It is merely the veil of straight time that is lifted from Orlando's face and body and heart. The physical change is the most jarringly obvious alteration, but is certainly not the only one, or even the deepest one; it is merely the one that is the most visible to the reader and is therefore the loudest signal to the reader that Orlando has now left straight time.

I would go so far as to say that Orlando never belonged in straight time. As the following excerpt will demonstrate, even prior to his transformation, Orlando is drawn to the potentiality within himself, a queer potentiality that, like Muñoz's 'crashing wave' (Muñoz, 2009, p. 185) of queerness, can no longer be resisted or denied and is inevitably borne out in Orlando's biological sex change. At the start of the novel, Orlando already shows signs of harbouring a bisexual attraction for another person, regardless of their sex:

> The person, whatever the name or sex, was about middle height, very slenderly fashioned, and dressed entirely in oyster-coloured velvet, trimmed with some unfamiliar greenish-coloured fur. But these details were obscured by the extraordinary seductiveness which issued from the whole person. (*Orlando*, ch. 1, par. 27)

This 'person' is revealed to be Sasha, who later becomes Orlando's first great love. Orlando's attraction to Sasha prior to discovering her sex indicates not only Orlando's nascent queerness in terms of sexuality, but also in terms of gender identity. It is my hypothesis that the ambiguity of Orlando's gender identity pre-dates its external manifestation; Orlando's journey from straight time to queer time begins far prior to Orlando's physical transformation. The scene just quoted, in which Sasha's androgyny appeals powerfully to Orlando, is an instance of foreshadowing. Sasha's appeal is as much a recognition of self as a recognition of other, or rather, it is the same recognition of other-as-self that so bewitched Narcissus when he glimpsed himself in a pond. This recognition of self parallels the Lacanian mirror stage (Lacan, 1986, pp. 734-738), which is considered pivotal in the development of the human psyche. Orlando must undergo his own textual mirror stage as a character before his deep, internal, subconscious recognition of his queerness ripples outward and changes his physical form. Sasha is Orlando's reflection in the proverbial mirror of the self, and is Orlando's first, mesmerising glimpse of who 'he' really is:

> He had indeed just brought his feet together about six in the evening of the seventh of January [...] when he beheld, coming from the pavilion of the Muscovite Embassy, a figure, which, whether boy's or woman's, for the loose tunic and trousers of the Russian fashion served to disguise the sex, filled him with the highest curiosity. [...] Images, metaphors of the most extreme and extravagant twined and twisted in his mind. He called her a melon, a pineapple, an olive tree, an emerald, and a fox in the snow all in the space of three seconds; he did not know whether

he had heard her, tasted her, seen her, or all three together. [...] As it was, he drew his lips up over his small white teeth; opened them perhaps half an inch as if to bite; shut them as if he had bitten. (*Orlando*, ch. 1, par. 27)

Orlando's first sighting of Sasha occurs in straight time, conspicuously and painstakingly noted as a clear linear progression from six to seven ('six in the evening of the seventh'), for until then, Orlando *was* in straight time—or thought he was. However, Sasha's appearance explodes straight time; her breathtaking androgyny explodes the male/female gender binary and also the past/future time binary. In scrambling for appropriately flattering phrases to describe her, Orlando becomes unmoored from his usual facility with words in describing and courting women; indeed, he becomes unmoored at a far deeper level, so much so that the totality of his experience of her—his *recognition* of her—goes beyond all the physical senses, in a synaesthetic burst of sensation. He wishes to 'bite' her, not merely carnally, but to imbibe the essence of *what she is*: that elfin, indefinable state beyond gender, so compellingly 'seductive' to Orlando because it contains the twofold seductiveness of both sexes.

Orlando is intoxicated not so much by Sasha herself, who he can never adequately describe and who, by his own admission, he does not truly understand—he repeatedly refers to her as 'something hidden,' 'something concealed' (*Orlando*, ch. 1, par. 39)—but what Sasha represents to him, a vision of himself that he has as yet not encountered, a glimpse of what he will become, a queer potentiality. Moreover, in an aside, the narrator informs the reader that Orlando's hyperbolic metaphors in describing Sasha, whose gender is as yet unknown, 'were mostly taken from the things he had liked the taste of as a boy' (*Orlando*, ch. 1, par. 27), hinting that Orlando's non-heterosexual tendencies may have been present since childhood. In the light of this aside, Orlando's desire for Sasha prior to the revelation of Sasha's womanhood suggests that Orlando may have always had bisexual leanings.

> When the boy, for alas, a boy it must be—no woman could skate with such speed and vigour—swept almost on tiptoe past him, Orlando was ready to tear his hair with vexation that the person was of his own sex, and thus all embraces were out of the question. But the skater came closer. Legs, hands, carriage, were a boy's, but no boy ever had a mouth like that; no boy had those breasts; no boy had eyes which looked as if they had been fished from the bottom of the sea. Finally [...] the unknown skater came to a standstill. She was not a handsbreadth off. She was a woman. (*Orlando*, ch. 1, par. 27)

Orlando has already begun 'his' departure from straight time, here. In thinking that Sasha is a man, Orlando bemoans not the fact that this sumptuous stranger is a man *and is therefore undesirable to him*, but that, socially, any sexual contact is 'out of the question.' This is a crucial distinction, even if Orlando, drowning in the overwhelming wonder of the moment, does not see it for the queer potentiality it is. The split between internal queer time (desire) and external straight time (convention) has already taken root in him, a crack that will eventually spread throughout his being and will result in the shattering of his 'male' shell. This will then lead to a bodily change that finally, fully extracts Orlando from straight time, and, in the eyes of society, allows him to pursue a romantic relationship with a man—Orlando's future husband, Shelmerdine. In the instant Orlando sees Sasha, he is as rapt as Narcissus at what, unbeknownst even to him, is a prophetic image of his innermost self. It is an image of genderfluidity that he himself will come to embody, a 'queer futurity' (Muñoz, 2009, p. 185) that is his soul's recognition of itself.

This incident takes place in the first chapter, and thus, Orlando's gender journey begins from the very start of the novel. His failed union with Sasha—*with his own potentiality*—drives him to sorrow and eventually into the coma that results in his change. Sasha fails to appear at the time they had agreed upon and, as the clock of St Paul's strikes 'the first stroke of midnight,' other clocks also strike all at once, 'jangling one after another,' together forming what, to Orlando, seems 'a voice full of horror and alarm' (*Orlando*, ch. 1, par. 56). This apocalyptic, cacophonic ringing of clocks marks the end of straight time for Orlando. These clocks, all based in straight time and marking the linear progression of hours, metaphorically possess, to Orlando's ears, a voice screaming in opposition to Orlando's true self. As the clocks ring, 'the sixth stroke echoed away, and the seventh came and the eighth, and to his apprehensive mind they seemed notes first heralding and then proclaiming death' (*Orlando*, ch. 1, par. 56)—not only the textual death of Orlando's relationship with Sasha, but the subtextual death of straight time and of Orlando's seemingly heterosexual, cisgender identity. The linear order of six to seven to eight is overturned altogether by the profundity of Orlando's trauma, of his loss of Sasha. That loss culminates in Orlando retiring 'to his great house in the country' and living 'there in complete solitude'; in his grief, he slips into 'a trance' from which he cannot be awoken (*Orlando*, ch. 2, par. 2). It is this supernatural sleep that eventually changes Orlando's sex, and it is Orlando's despair at losing Sasha that instigates the first textual example of such a sleep, which facilitates the death of Orlando's straight, cisgender identity by permitting Orlando to 'take death in small doses' (*Orlando*, ch. 2, par. 3) until that death is completed in his physical metamorphosis into a woman.

On the surface, it is Orlando's heartbreak at Sasha's abandonment of him that so wounds him. More deeply, it is the temporal and spatial distance between Orlando and his own queerness that his distance from Sasha metaphorises, and which Orlando mourns. This distance between appearance and self is only bridged when Orlando crosses over into queer time and into a body that, in a sense, turns him *into* Sasha. Becoming Sasha is a union more complete than the one he had hoped for when he had waited fruitlessly for her as the clocks of straight time had announced the end of his masculinity. Orlando does not realise that his desire for Sasha's androgynous beauty is a sublimation of his own innate desire for self-completion, for the wholeness of being both 'he' and 'she' that his change finally allows him to experience. Failing an outward fusion with Sasha— or rather, with what Sasha represents—Orlando finds an inward fusion instead, which is perhaps the fusion he was always seeking, a fusion between 'Love['s] two faces; one white, the other black; two bodies; one smooth, the other hairy,' which are 'joined together' so 'strictly […] that you cannot separate them' (*Orlando*, ch. 2, par. 69). Indeed, it is only after transforming physically into a woman and mentally into a fused, genderfluid entity that Orlando finds herself truly capable of understanding Sasha as a person and not merely as an extension or representation of Orlando's self:

> Now, the obscurity, which divides the sexes and lets linger innumerable impurities in its gloom, was removed, and if there is anything in what the poet says about truth and beauty, this affection gained in beauty what it lost in falsity. At last, she cried, she knew Sasha as she was [...]
> (*Orlando*, ch. 4, par. 11)

After 'her' sex change, and from the vantage point of her newly ambiguous gender identity, Orlando finally feels as though she understands Sasha, who she could not understand before. Orlando's enhanced insight is not only a simplistic case of them both now being physically women; Orlando's understanding of herself in queer time is deeper than it was in straight time. That 'which divides the sexes' is gone from *within* Orlando, as well; the heteronormativity of the gender binary no longer holds sway over Orlando's psyche, or at least, no longer utterly confines it. This interpretation of the text is borne out by the passage signaling Orlando's transformation:

> The trumpeters, ranging themselves side by side in order, blow one terrific blast:—'THE TRUTH! . . . at which Orlando woke. He stretched himself. He rose. He stood upright in complete nakedness before us, and while the trumpets pealed Truth! Truth! Truth! we have no choice left but confess — he was a woman. (*Orlando*, ch. 3, pars. 37-40)

Orlando's transformation is his truth, or his body's expression of his truth. Even though his new body is a 'female' body and not an intersex form, it nonetheless allows Orlando to contain and express genderfluidity experientially and psychologically, by occupying a liminal, genderfluid mental space where 'man' and 'woman' intermingle. Orlando's phenomenological continuity and generally unchanging personality, regardless of physical sex, allows Orlando to reflect on manhood and womanhood from a space that contains them both. Yet there is also a drive—an opposing external force—attempting to push back at Orlando's gender identity. Just before Orlando's transformation, as quoted in the passage above, Orlando's 'truth' is urged by straight time to continue hiding itself in the closet:

> Truth come not out from your horrid den. Hide deeper, fearful Truth. For you flaunt in the brutal gaze of the sun things that were better unknown and undone; you unveil the shameful; the dark you make clear, Hide! Hide! Hide! (*Orlando*, ch. 3, par. 28)

And yet, the truth does not hide, nor does it submit to the accusation of being 'shameful.' Orlando awakens forever changed, her altered body itself now a queer chronotope, an embodiment of queer time. Orlando's transformation is unstoppable by straight time precisely because it is the truth, and the truth cannot be stopped, suppressed or silenced… at least not for long. Straight time must ultimately submit to the 'crashing wave' (Muñoz, 2009, p. 185) of queerness, the truth of which conquers all attempts by social convention to contain it. By living through centuries of straight time and remaining untouched by it (i.e. not succumbing to its linear directionality towards death), the immortal Orlando now occupies a state 'of being outside of oneself in time,' a queer time that has 'a sense of timelessness's motion, comprehending a temporal unity, which includes the past (having-been), the future (the not-yet), and the present (the making-present)' (Muñoz, 2009, p. 186). Orlando's having-been manhood and making-present womanhood hint at a not-yet genderfluidity that, though it is already embodied by Orlando, is not specifically referenced within the text using non-binary pronouns. Yet the lack of non-binary pronouns does not detract overmuch from the text's genderqueerness, given that Orlando herself is the overarching 'temporal unity' unifying these differently gendered selves.

Gender Lag

Straight time is linear, monodirectional and deterministic, while queer time is non-linear, multidirectional and non-deterministic. Orlando, despite having the benefit of experiencing both sexes, does not favour either more than the other. She criticises both sexes without prejudice:

> And here it would seem from some ambiguity in her terms that she was censuring both sexes equally, as if she belonged to neither; and indeed, for the time being, she seemed to vacillate; she was man; she was woman; she knew the secrets, shared the weaknesses of each […] Thus it is no great wonder, as she pitted one sex against the other, and found each alternately full of the most deplorable infirmities, [that she] was not sure to which she belonged […] (*Orlando*, ch. 4, par. 8)

This uncertainty suggests a genderfluidity within Orlando. In the novel, gender is depicted as osmotic, not only as something essential and inborn or as something willfully performed, but as something that also, in part, filters in from the outside as a result of social conditioning. Orlando's new tendency to blush (*Orlando*, ch. 5, par. 4) and faint from mortification (*Orlando*, ch. 4, par. 32) are not tendencies that were present in her when she was a man, nor evident in her immediately after becoming a woman. While Orlando is always quintessentially Orlando, there are certainly new behavioural and functional traits that are associated with the gender performance of her newly acquired womanhood. These traits are slowly accrued by Orlando through an automatic, unselfconscious social mimesis, but they are acquired habits and are by no means innate.

This 'gender lag,' if I may term it thus, is due to what Orlando calls 'the culpable laggardry of the human frame,' that is, the existence of a temporal distance between biological sex and gender identity. After waking in a female body, Orlando's thoughts show that Orlando's transition into the female gender lags somewhat behind the transformation of her body into the 'female' sex, and that her new gender, with its attendant social connotations and conventions, is still catching up with her:

'Ignorant and poor as we are compared with the other sex,' she thought [...] and from these opening words it is plain that something had happened during the night to give her a push towards the female sex, for she was speaking more as a woman speaks than as a man, yet with a sort of content after all. [...] And as all Orlando's loves had been women, now, through the culpable laggardry

of the human frame to adapt itself to convention, though
she herself was a woman, it was still a woman she loved;
and if the consciousness of being of the same sex had any
effect at all, it was to quicken and deepen those feelings
which she had had as a man. (*Orlando*, ch. 4, pars. 10-11)

The lesbian subtext here is clear; Orlando is now a woman
who loves women, although she is not yet fully a woman in
her mind. Rather, even though her body has transformed,
her mind lags behind, and though she speaks 'more as a
woman […] than as a man,' she is still somewhat, in terms
of her fluid gender identity, a man. As a result, Orlando's
'laggardry,' while used to illumine the non-immutability of
the biology-gender equivalency, is also used as an excuse
to explain away—or conceal—Orlando's queerness. The
incompleteness of Orlando's inner transformation into
womanhood is cited as the root of her continuing longing
for women, a queer longing that is gradually overtaken
within the text, if not outright erased, as Orlando becomes
more womanly and her erstwhile passion for women is
subsumed by desire for a man, albeit a man who is less
overtly masculine, like her beloved Shelmerdine: 'a man
as strange and subtle as a woman' (*Orlando*, ch. 5, par. 56).
Eventually, the relationship dynamic that prevails is
seemingly a heterosexual one, albeit somewhat non-standard
in its particulars, in that the woman used to be a man, and
that the man, apparently, is much like a woman. It can be
argued that the relationship is a queer one, particularly if
Orlando is seen as genderqueer and bisexual, and her partner
as at least partly gender non-conforming, but to the straight
gaze (the censor's gaze), it will likely still appear to be a
straight relationship. Thus, queerness is both subtextually

hinted at as a 'potentiality' (Muñoz, 2009, p. 185) while being outwardly and textually denied. Vital as this denial may have been for the text's survival under the censorship of its era, as previously described in the section titled 'Cultural Context,' it nevertheless detracts from the broader acceptance of queerness and non-heteronormativity within the text, and consequently within the reader. Whether this is a necessary evil born entirely of censorship or an authorial decision for other reasons remains subject to debate, but Woolf's awareness of the threat of a court trial must be considered in any queer analysis of the text.

The 'gender lag' within the text *does* link biological sex to gender identity, in the sense that Orlando's pronouns change to 'she/her' immediately after her sex change, even if her psychology does not entirely catch up. However, the narrative also suggests that if gender identity lags behind biology, then gender may not be entirely innate, but a coalescence of nature and nurture. That gender identity is still tethered to biological sex, albeit lagging somewhat behind it, partly reinforces the heteronormative ideal that equates gender with sex at birth, even as the lag also suggests that there is room for gender alterity and sexual diversity. This is not a complete debunking of heteronormativity, but Orlando makes considerable headway into unhitching gender identity at least partially from biological sex, and it does so through entering queer time.

The House Outside Time

Orlando's house at Blackfriars is in a continuous state of pause, and remains so while the straight world (and straight time) proceeds without it. As Makiko Minow-Pinkney says, 'the great country house and estate successfully totalises Orlando's many part-selves,' and '[t]he house is origin and continuity, the origin as continuity' (Minow-Pinkney, 1985, p. 225), its continuity being a resistance of the ordered divisibility of straight time. Orlando's house, with its three-hundred-and-sixty-five rooms and fifty-two staircases, is clearly a metaphor for time itself. The house's design is a system of measurement that seems to follow the linear conventions of straight time, but is actually subversive, for the house retains its internal structures regardless of the outside forces of history and society. This queer coding of internal reality versus external illusion metaphorises the queer experience of living in the closet, which on the inside exists in queer time while outwardly appearing to conform to straight time.

This discrepancy is a different sort of lag than the aforementioned gender lag; it is an example of what I call 'closet lag,' wherein the social reality presented or performed in the outside world is at odds with or lags behind the experiential reality of queerness within one's own mind. While seemingly oppressive, the mind-space of the closet nonetheless emphasises queer agency in that only the queer agent can choose if or how to present or accept their queerness externally or internally. It is also an inviolable 'safe space' where the agent can be unabashedly (if internally) queer. Orlando's house is a safe space, a queer space, inasmuch as it is an expression of Orlando's queer agency. Only Orlando can affect change in this house— in this *body*—that exists out of straight time. The house is a spatiotemporal metaphor for Orlando's body, and any changes in it are a direct result of Orlando's queer agency, just as any changes that do not occur in it are a result of Orlando's queer resistance to straight time. It is Orlando's own decision to refurnish the house that precedes 'his' sex change, and as the narrator remarks, '[i]t was a change in Orlando herself that dictated her choice of a woman's dress and of a woman's sex' (*Orlando*, ch. 4, pars. 51-52), indicating that the change is of Orlando's own will.

Thus, the transformation of Orlando's body parallels the transformation of Orlando's house, combining them into a unified chronotope. The house, as an 'individual interior dwelling,' is not only a physical interior but a *psychological* interior. It signifies Orlando's internal closet that 'becomes a space of queer possibility and reenaction […] Waiting here means being out of time, or at least out of a linear mapping that is straight time' (Muñoz, 2009, p. 182). Orlando enters into her house in order to get out of the 'linear mapping that is straight time.' Her house exists in the same protective pause that Orlando was under while transforming; it is an extension of the pupa's protective husk, wherein, sheltered from the external spatiotemporal forces that comprise straight time, the queer inner self can evolve.

Orlando's home is a depiction of the closet as a safehouse rather than a cage, as a continuous resistance of rather than a containment by straight time. In *Orlando*, the closet becomes an internal space of empowerment and agency rather than an impoverishment of both, and is a rebel armory and/or hideout that provides means of protection and tactical retreat from the war constantly waged upon queerness by society.

A Queer Metamorphosis

'*Queering* enacts a move from categorising noun to continuous, changing verb' (Ryan, 2013, p. 108), and Orlando's genderqueer body is certainly a changing verb, just as Orlando's ever-evolving gender identity (which is still in the process of changing at the end of the novel) is in continuous evolution. This near-Nietzschean 'eternal recurrence' of queerness is represented in *Orlando* by the 'continual stopping and resetting of the clock of history' (Baucom, 2001, p. 160), i.e. the resetting of the clock of straight time, of which Orlando's physical transformation is but one instance. This resetting continues whenever straight time seeks to declare an arbitrary boundary between past and future and to thereby reaffirm the time binary and the gender binary. Orlando continuously resists this function of straight time. For example, upon 'the twelfth stroke of midnight' (*Orlando*, ch. 4, par. 101) that announces the turn of the nineteenth century, Orlando resists its onset by retreating to her timeless home in Blackfriars, which exists in another dimension altogether—the spatiotemporal dimension of queer time.

Queer time becomes possible when the 'established temporal order' of straight time 'gets interrupted and new encounters consequently take place' (Freeman, 2010, p. xxii). In *Orlando* the interruption is Orlando's long sleep, which freezes Orlando's subjective time and provides Orlando with a transformative mechanism that naturalises the process of Orlando's sex change, and that therefore also naturalises Orlando's queerness, inviting readers to suspend their disbelief of both. This sleep-as-transformation trope once again mirrors the natural phenomenon of the pupa's transformation into a butterfly, and the more fantastical fable of Sleeping Beauty, wherein 'sleep is the soul-saviour that protects her inner self while her body passes through metamorphosis' (Gould, 2006, p. 92), just as the shell of the pupa protects that which sleeps within it.

Queerness as metamorphosis—and queer time as an ongoing metamorphosal temporality without beginning or end—is signified by Orlando's long life and Orlando's enduring spirit, which, at the end of the novel, is still undergoing transformations that are internal, if not external as Orlando's sex change was. Orlando, as the novel progresses, becomes comfortably genderqueer both in mind and in presentation, and changes 'frequently from one set of clothes to another,' exchanging 'the probity of breeches' for 'the seductiveness of petticoats,' with 'no difficulty in sustaining the different parts' (*Orlando*, ch. 4, par. 97). Like a genderfluid trickster spirit (Bassil-Morozow, 2017, p. 93), Orlando now shifts seamlessly from male to female guises, and thus enjoys the best of both worlds, reaping 'a twofold harvest' and enjoying 'the love of both sexes equally' (*Orlando*, ch. 4, par. 97). Orlando's genderfluidity and apparent bisexuality become ever-bolder as she travels deeper into queer time, and the vacillation of her gender performativity between that of the sexes is evidence of 'the power of androgyny to queer a text' (Paludi, 2012, p. 184). Even if no non-binary pronouns are applied to Orlando within the text, Orlando is clearly non-binary and presents as such. 'Her' gender performance flits, sprite-like, from male to female and back, and she is just as comfortable in the in-between spaces between genders as she is within the genders themselves. Indeed, in her androgyny, Orlando not only deconstructs the gender binary but often occupies, to her confused admirers, *both* genders, much as Sasha's androgyny had muddled an amorous Orlando at first sight.

As discussed earlier in this chapter, Orlando's meeting with Sasha marked the beginning of Orlando's departure from straight time. Now, as both man and woman who is attractive to both men and women, Orlando's queer time continues to destabilise straight time, not only in herself but in other people. Orlando's genderfluidity is not only an expression of queer time, but an invitation to *others* to leave straight time; queer time is 'seductive' just as Sasha's (and now Orlando's) androgyny is. Just as Sasha drew Orlando into queer time, so it is implied that Orlando may be drawing others, such as the Archduke/Archduchess, into queer time, into an irresistible orbit around herself in which she acts as the gravitational force that attracts others to queer time, that incites others to question heteronormativity and the male/female gender binary.

'Queer subcultures produce alternative temporalities by allowing their participants to believe that their futures can be imagined according to the logics that lie outside of those paradigmatic markers of life experience—namely, birth, marriage, reproduction, and death' (Halberstam, 2005, p. 2). *Orlando* resists these 'paradigmatic markers' by taking death out of the equation for its seemingly immortal protagonist, and by flouting the heteronormative gender determinism of birth. Heterosexual reproduction is wholly absent from the narrative; the linear, non-negotiable origin of birth is replaced instead by a queer *rebirth*, a non-binary self-perpetuation in which Orlando effectively re-creates herself as another gender and sex. Orlando's transformation turns birth into a cyclical, non-linear phenomenon that can be returned to and revisioned, and this queer rebirth subverts the heteronormative concept of birth as a one-time-only event, immutable and unchangeable. Even the one official marriage that takes place—between Orlando and Shelmerdine—has queer undertones in that Orlando is a genderfluid bisexual who was once biologically a man, and that Shelmerdine, too, is an unconventional man who is 'as strange and subtle as a woman' (*Orlando*, ch. 5, par. 56) and who may therefore be genderqueer. The novel queers each of the 'paradigmatic markers' of straight time.

Freeman defines standard linear temporality, or straight time, as 'a mode of implantation through which institutional forces,' such as heteronormativity, 'come to seem like somatic facts' (Freeman, 2007, p. 160). 'Queer time resists such "facts"' (Micir, 2019, p. 353), and queerness constitutes both 'pressure against the state's naming apparatus, particularly against the normalizing taxonomies of male and female, heterosexual and homosexual,' and pressure against '*periodizing* apparatuses' (Freeman, 2005, p. 58). Woolf resists the periodising apparatus of the unchanging, straight, binary-gendered body by creating a changing, queer, non-binary-gendered body, and does so through the text's 'consistent resistance to modernity's standard time' (Micir, 2019, p. 353), i.e. straight time. The following passage occurs prior to Orlando's transformation but still addresses Orlando's resistance to straight time:

> It would be no exaggeration to say that he would go out after breakfast a man of thirty and come home to dinner

a man of fifty-five at least. Some weeks added a century to his age, others no more than three seconds at most. Altogether, the task of estimating the length of human life […] is beyond our capacity, for directly we say that it is ages long, we are reminded that it is briefer than the fall of a rose leaf to the ground. Of the two forces which alternately, and what is more confusing still, at the same moment, dominate our unfortunate numbskulls—brevity and diuturnity—Orlando was sometimes under the influence of the elephant-footed deity, then of the gnat-winged fly. Life seemed to him of prodigious length. Yet even so, it went like a flash. (*Orlando*, ch. 2, par. 38)

Orlando resists straight time by concurrently occupying the temporal states of 'brevity and diuturnity.' He blurs the border between those states, such that their seeming binary opposition is deconstructed and they are revealed to be two sides of the same coin, defining each other and dependent on each other. The above quote demonstrates that even before his transition into a woman's body, Orlando experiences life through the non-linearity of queer time. He resists the 'facts' of the countable, discrete and linear structures of straight time—the hours, days, months, years and centuries—by occupying some, all or none of them simultaneously. It is no wonder, then, that in his resistance to straight time's 'periodising apparatuses,' Orlando eventually comes to occupy some, all or none of the genders as well.

Another resistance to straight time occurs through the text's usage of standard fairytale parlance, not only in reference to Orlando's metamorphosal, Sleeping Beauty-esque sleep, but also in reference to time itself, particularly the Cinderella-like transformational time of the 'stroke of

midnight' (*Orlando*, ch. 4, par. 101), during which many
of the pivotal changes in Orlando's life occur. Indeed, the
phrase 'stroke of midnight' occurs no less than seven times
during the course of the novel, be it when it marks Sasha's
abandonment of Orlando, or Shelmerdine's penultimate
arrival, or Orlando's return to Blackfriars at the turn of
the nineteenth century and the twentieth. Each such stroke
signals some aspect of Orlando's queer emergence, and
indicates some element of Orlando's departure from straight
time. These strokes of midnight indicate the crossing-over
boundary between straight time and queer time, between
the time of the rational (linear) and the time of the magical
(non-linear). This persistent narrative counter-current
against straight time creates a textual queer riptide that
pulls the reader in the opposite direction of the prevailing
heteronormative paradigm. Not only that, but given that
Orlando's first sex change occurred without warning, there
is no guarantee that another transformation may not be
just around the corner. After all, the metamorphosis that is
queerness is ongoing, and the stroke of midnight is bound
to recur.

Transgender Connotations

Even after her sex change, Orlando's genderfluidity
continues to present itself diversely, be it through breeches
or skirts or some androgynous amalgam of the two. The
following description of Orlando's transformation as
painless is progressive and trans-positive; it is not painful
or punitive, punishing Orlando's queerness as the queerness
of the tragic protagonist of Radclyffe Hall's *The Well of*

Loneliness was punished, despite that novel being published in 1928, the very same year as *Orlando*.

> The change seemed to have been accomplished painlessly and completely and in such a way that Orlando herself showed no surprise at it. Many people, taking this into account, and holding that such a change of sex is against nature, have been at great pains to prove (1) that Orlando had always been a woman, (2) that Orlando is at this moment a man. Let biologists and psychologists determine. (*Orlando*, ch. 3, par. 41)

The painlessness of Orlando's transition is the transgender ideal, and the narrator of the novel implies that 'such a change of sex' is not, in fact, 'against nature.' Indeed, Orlando's transformation is not punished in any way in the novel, either through physical or psychological pain. The narrator also acknowledges that the majority of heteronormative society vehemently opposes this sort of change and insists, largely in order to preserve its own default primacy and privilege, that cisgender perpetuity (Orlando was 'always' one or the other gender) exists and is universal, and that nobody is exempt from it. Orlando unapologetically exempts herself from that rule.

The asynchrony between a post-transition Orlando's inner state and the cultural customs of whichever time she happens to be living in contributes to the deconstruction of straight time, as is evidenced by her relatively permissive attitude to gender performance compared to the nineteenth century she finds herself in: 'While this went on in every part of England, it was all very well for Orlando to mew herself in her house at Blackfriars and pretend that the climate was

the same; that one could still say what one liked and wear
knee-breeches or skirts as the fancy took one' (*Orlando*, ch.
5, par. 4). Orlando's queer resistance to the linear march of
straight time is crucial to the text's deconstruction not only
of the past/future time binary, but of the male/female gender
binary. This, of course, also leads to Orlando being both
a living anachronism and a living prophecy, by virtue of
being a historical throwback who is nonetheless strangely
progressive. After her transition, Orlando is constantly out
of (straight) time in one sense or another, be it in her gender
performativity or in her beliefs about the sexes. This, too,
has transgender connotations, in that there is often a similar
mismatch between the social conventions of gender and the
transgender individual's gender identity and performativity.

The central anastrophe of the text is the internal,
psychological, queer inversion of the usual heteronormative
order of biological sex and gender identity, suggesting that
the latter may potentially pre-date the former. Straight time
dictates that biological sex determines gender identity,
but queer time (and the narrator of Orlando) suggests the
opposite. As the novel's narrator says, 'It was a change in
Orlando herself that dictated her choice of a woman's dress
and of a woman's sex' (*Orlando*, ch. 4, par. 51). Thus, while
Orlando's sex change *seems* to occur out of nowhere and
to lack agency, it is implied that, at least subconsciously,
Orlando made a choice at some point—that within Orlando
lay a genderqueer and/or transgender identity that must be
understood in order to wholly appreciate Orlando's apparent
reincarnation, which may not be a reincarnation at all but
a closer expression of what had always been her gender
identity. Thus, as discussed previously in this chapter,

Orlando's transformation may not simply be an external one, but one in which Orlando's internal metamorphosis results in an external change. In this, *Orlando* is essentially a transgender origin myth, for if Orlando's transformation is 'presented as 'she' becoming 'she' ,' then it 'cannot be linked to a sexual metamorphosis within an oppositional binary framework' (Ryan, 2013, p. 104), that is, within the framework of cisgenderism. Instead, if Orlando's transformation is a case of '"she" becoming "she,"' then it may signal a transgender *return to self* rather than a cisgender departure from self. Such a reading is possible because Orlando's transformation 'becomes circular' (Minow-Pinkney qtd. in Ryan 2013, p. 104) and in so doing thwarts the linearity of straight time. Orlando's seeming metamorphosis is therefore not a simple binary switch from male to female, but a recursion of genderqueer returning to genderqueer, in cyclical, queer time.

This viewpoint is, in essence, the difference between the heteronormative term 'gender reassignment surgery' and the far more trans-positive 'gender confirmation surgery' (Schechter, 2016, p. par. 2), for such a surgery *confirms* a transgender person's gender identity; it does not reassign it or reinvent it. The inversion of straight time—which insists on the pre-eminence and 'firstness' of biological sex in determining gender identity—leads here to a subtextual acknowledgment of the individual's own gender identity as the deciding factor, not biology. It is Orlando's gender identity that determines the sex change she undergoes, not vice-versa. The linear timeline of sex-at-birth cisgenderism is de-sequenced and reclaimed by Orlando as a transgender figure.

Conclusion

The character of Orlando is the personification of Woolf's 'radical reformulation of time and chronology' (Lojo-Rodríguez, 2019, p. 470). Orlando is a queer chronotope that deconstructs the heteronormative gender binary and resists the cisgender bias inherent in that binary, by refusing to have 'always been a woman' or being 'at this moment a man' (*Orlando*, ch. 3, par. 42). Orlando defies the heteronormative narrative of straight time that casts 'such a change of sex' (*Orlando*, ch. 3, par. 42) as unnatural, that seeks to flatten Orlando's multifaceted, genderfluid identity into one or the other, male or female.

Instead, Orlando is a trans-positive, genderfluid hero(ine) who crosses the limits of straight time and emerges into queer time as unabashedly genderqueer. While no non-binary pronouns are used to refer to Orlando, and while much of the queer subtext remains couched in heteronormative language that maintains the basic, archetypal precept of two opposing sexes ('[d]ifferent though the sexes are,' as the narrator affirms in chapter four), the novel nonetheless suggests that *gender*—separate from biological sex—need not subscribe to the same binary model, or not to the same extent. Orlando's textual presentation remains enduringly non-binary, and ripe for revisioning through the contemporary queer lens.

References

Abel, E. (1989) *Virginia Woolf and the Fictions of Psychoanalysis*. Chicago: University of Chicago Press.

Bakhtin, M. (1981) 'Forms of time and of the chronotope in the novel' in Holquist, M. (ed.) *The Dialogic Imagination*. Austin: Texas University Press.

Bassil-Morotzow, H. (2017) 'Loki then and now: the trickster against civilization,' *International Journal of Jungian Studies*, 9(2), pp. 84-96.

Baucom, I. (2001) 'Globalit, Inc.; or, The Cultural Logic of Global Literary Studies,' *PMLA*, 116(1), pp. 158-172.

Bell, Q. (1972) *Mrs Woolf: 1912-1941, Volume 2*. London: Hogarth Press.

Brown, E.H. (2019) *Work!: A Queer History of Modeling*. Durham: Duke University Press.

Derry, C. (2018) 'Lesbianism and Feminist Legislation in 1921: the Age of Consent and "Gross Indecency between Women,"' *History Workshop Journal*, 86, pp. 245-267.

Edwards, J. (2009) *Eve Kosofsky Sedgwick*. New York: Routledge.

Freeman, E. (2005) 'Time Binds, or Erotohistoriography,' *Social Text*, 23, pp. 57-68.
---. (2007) 'Introduction.' *GLQ: A Journal of Lesbian and Gay Studies*, 13(2-3), pp. 159-176.
---. (2010) Time Binds: Queer Temporalities, Queer Histories. Durham: Duke University Press.

Gould, J. (2006) *Spinning Straw into Gold: What Fairy Tales Reveal About the Transformations in a Woman's Life*. New York: Random House.

Halberstam, J. (2005) *In a Queer Time and Space*. New York: New York University Press.

Hall, R. (1928) *The Well of Loneliness*. London: Jonathan Cape.

Hankins, L.K. (1997) '*Orlando*: "A Precipice Marked V": Between "A Miracle of Discretion" and "Lovemaking Unbelievable: Indiscretions Incredible"' in, Barrett E. and Cramer, P. (eds.) *Virginia Woolf: Lesbian Readings*. New York: New York University Press, pp. 180-202.

Jagose, A. (2002) *Inconsequence: Lesbian Representation and the Logic of Sexual Sequence*. Ithaca: Cornell University Press.

Lacan, J. (1986) 'The Mirror Stage' in Adams, H. and Searle, L (eds.) *Critical Theory Since 1965*. Gainesville: Florida State University Press, pp. 734-738.

Lewis, M. (2008) *Derrida and Lacan: Another Writing*. Edinburgh: Edinburgh University Press.

Lojo-Rodríguez, L.M. (2019) 'Woolf in Hispanic Countries: Buenos Aires and Madrid' in Berman, J. (ed.) *A Companion to Virginia Woolf*. New Jersey: Wiley Blackwell, pp. 467-480.

Micir, M. (2019) 'Queer Woolf' in Berman, J. (ed.) *A Companion to Virginia Woolf*. New Jersey: Wiley Blackwell, pp. 347-358.

Minow-Pinkney, M. (1985) 'Feminine Writing and the Problem of the Self: an Examination of Virginia Woolf's Novels in the Light of Recent Critical and Psychoanalytic Theories.' PhD Thesis. University of Warwick. Available at: <http://wrap.warwick.ac.uk/4406/> (Accessed 26 October 2019).

Muñoz, J.E. (2009) *Cruising Utopia: The Then and There of Queer Futurity*. New York: New York University Press.

Paludi, M.A. (2012) *The Psychology of Love: Volume 1*. California: Praeger.

Ryan, D. (2013) *Virginia Woolf and the Materiality of Theory: Sex, Animal, Life*. Edinburgh: Edinburgh University Press.

Sackville-West, V. (1974) *Challenge*. New York: Avon Books.

Schechter, L.S. (2016) '"Gender Confirmation Surgery": What's in a Name?,' *Huffpost*, 2 February [online]. Available at: <https://www.huffpost.com/entry/gender-confirmation-surgery_b_1442262> (Accessed 26 October 2019).

Sedgwick, E.K. (2013) 'Queer and Now' in Hall, D.E., Jagose, A., Bebell, A. and Potter, S. (eds.) *The Routledge Queer Studies Reader*. New York: Routledge, pp. 3-17.

Smorag, P. (2008) 'From Closet Talk to PC Terminology: Gay Speech and the Politics of Visibility,' *Transatlantica*, 1, 14 May [online]. Available at: <http://journals.openedition.org/transatlantica/3503> (Accessed 26 October 2019).

Stanley, L. (2014) *Sex Surveyed, 1949-1994: From Mass-Observation's 'Little Kinsey' to the National Survey and the Hite Reports*. New York: Routledge.

Vanita, R. (1997) 'Bringing Buried Things to Light: Homoerotic Alliances in *To the Lighthouse*' in Barrett, E. and Cramer, P. (eds.) *Virginia Woolf: Lesbian Readings*. New York: New York University Press, pp. 165-179.

Woolf, V. (2003) *A Writer's Diary*. Edited by Leonard Woolf. California: Harcourt.

Woolf, V. (2015) *Orlando: A Biography. EBooks@Adelaide* [online]. Available at: <https://ebooks.adelaide.edu.au/w/woolf/virginia/w91o/complete.html> (Accessed 26 October 2019).

CHAPTER TWO

The Queer Time Machine in Robert A. Heinlein's 'All You Zombies'

[G]ender is trouble: Gender may trouble every imaginable
social relation and fuel every imaginable social hierarchy;
it may also threaten to undo itself and us with it.
— A. Finn Enke, *Transfeminist Perspectives*.

Introduction

Unlike *Orlando*, in which queerness exists as a potentiality,
Robert A. Heinlein's science fiction story 'All You Zombies'
(2018) features queerness front-and-centre in the form of its
canonically intersex protagonist. However, even here, that
queerness is wrapped in layers of 'straight time' (Muñoz,
2009, p. 25), layers that must be painstakingly deconstructed
through time travel.

Heinlein's 'All You Zombies,' initially published in
1959, is a short story that uses time travel as a literary
device to explore notions of identity, including gender
identity and sexuality. In it, the protagonist discovers and
ensures, through time travel, that s/he is their own mother
and father. The narrator is the Bartender, a time agent who
recruits his younger self, the Unmarried Mother, to be a

time agent as well. The Unmarried Mother is a young man who pens confession stories for a living from a woman's point of view, because he was once a woman named Jane who gave birth to a child outside of wedlock, and then, after being diagnosed as intersex, was forced to undergo gender reassignment surgery to change her biological sex into a man's—*not* gender confirmation surgery, as it was non-consensual. Jane, in turn, only bears her child after being impregnated by her own future, post-transition, male self (i.e. by the Unmarried Mother), and the child Jane gives birth to then grows up to be Jane, the Unmarried Mother and, ultimately, the Bartender. The climax of the story occurs when the reader realises that all the characters are, in fact, the same.

> Now you know who he is—and after you think it over you'll know who you are… and if you think hard enough, you'll figure out who the baby is… and who I am. (AYZ, par. 136)[1]

It is the reader's epiphany that the protagonist has been a man, a woman *and* intersex that dismantles the gender binary, and it is time travel that enables such a dismantling to occur, by merging the differently-gendered narrative arcs of Jane, the Unmarried Mother and the Bartender into the timeline of a single, non-binary narrator. This chapter examines how intersexuality, the language registers of detective fiction, the gender discrepancies of work, and the queer implications of self-perpetuation are used to disrupt both time and the

---

1. 'All You Zombies' will be shortened to AYZ in all subsequent in-text citations.

heteronormative gender binary in 'All You Zombies.'

Before launching into an in-depth analysis of the text, I must first locate it in Heinlein's prolific oeuvre of science fiction stories. Among the plethora of Heinlein's works on time travel are *For Us, the Living: A Comedy of Customs* (1939/2003), 'By His Bootstraps' (1941), 'Elsewhen' (1941), *The Door into Summer* (1957), *Farnham's Freehold* (1964), *Time Enough for Love* (1973), *The Number of the Beast* (1980), *The Cat Who Walks Through Walls* (1985) and *To Sail Beyond the Sunset* (1987). However, while these stories feature paradoxes and doppelgängers, just as 'All You Zombies' does, they do not engage explicitly with gender identity and queerness. Conversely, while works such as Heinlein's *Red Planet* (1949), *Stranger in a Strange Land* (1961), *I Will Fear No Evil* (1970) and *Friday* (1982) allude to queerness, they do not engage with it through time travel. Only 'All You Zombies' does both, which is why I selected this particular Heinlein text to focus on.[2] My aim is to unpack how time and gender are linked in this story, and how the deconstruction of binary time also deconstructs binary genders and sexualities, in effect queering the text.

This queering is accomplished via the conversion of 'straight time' (Muñoz, 2009, p. 25) into queer time, with a time machine being used as the mechanism for that conversion. '[S]traight time' is a linear, ordered model of time based on the time binary of past/future and before/after,

---

2. It should be noted that there is an Australian film adaptation of the story, released in 2014 and titled *Predestination*, directed by Michael Spierig and Peter Spierig, and starring Ethan Hawke. However, as the film does not adhere wholly to the plot of 'All You Zombies,' this chapter focuses solely on the original story and not on its film adaptation.

which leads to a linear model of gender and sexuality as well, since the time binary forms the foundation of the system of 'binarisms,' including gender and sexual binarisms, to which much of Western society subscribes (Bruhm, 2001, p. 15). In essence, the time binary reinforces the gender binary, and the deconstruction of the former contributes to the deconstruction of the latter. Upon escaping 'the temporal stranglehold' (Muñoz, 2009, p. 32) of straight time, we arrive at queer time, 'a queer temporality' that defies 'linear logic' (Muñoz, 2009, p. 186, p. 179). 'All You Zombies' is a narratological exploration of this phenomenon, in which the protagonist is a living 'chronotope' (Bakhtin, 1981, p. 84), an expression of how time (i.e. the protagonist's passage through the time machine) and space (i.e. the protagonist's changing body) are corporealised in the story's narrative. The queerness of 'All You Zombies' is, in turn, corporealised in its intersex protagonist. This queerness is not immediately apparent, but emerges from the story's continuous deconstruction of the gender binary.

As Heinlein said of his novel, *Stranger in a Stranger Land* (1961), which dealt with queer themes, the book was intended to confront 'the two biggest, fattest sacred cows of all, the two that every writer is supposed to give at least lip service to: the implicit assumptions of our Western culture concerning religion and sex' (Heinlein, 1989, p. 228). It can be inferred that 'All You Zombies,' which was published only two years prior, was written with a similar authorial intention to challenge assumptions regarding sex and sexuality. Even today, 'Heinlein's sexual rhetoric remains progressive and emblematic of human freedom' (Rochelle, 1999, p. 58).

The 'sexual rhetoric' of 'All You Zombies' addresses multiple queer issues, including intersex agency, sex at birth versus gender identity, and self-perpetuation by means other than heteronormative reproduction. I have therefore chosen to conduct a queer reading of the text. Heinlein biographer Farah Mendelsohn says of the author that '[h]e understood science fiction as part of the historical process and as part of preparing for the future' (2019, p. 7); if so, then 'All You Zombies' can be read as a preparation for a 'queer futurity' (Muñoz, 2009, p. 185), a preparation in which the strictures of heteronormativity are partly undone, hinting at the potential for further such unravellings.

If, as the gender theorist Morgan Holmes says, '*all* gender is trouble' (2008, p. 14), and, as transfeminist A. Finn Enke says, '*everyone*'s gender is made' (2012, p. 1), then Heinlein's short story is a seminal example of gender as manufactured trouble. Whether self-made as an expression of gender performance, or other-made as an enforcement of social conventions, a core theme of 'All You Zombies' is the invention of gender and its troubling of selfhood as temporal continuity. If anything, gender is used in this story to disrupt time, specifically straight time. The multiplicity of time loops within 'All You Zombies' achieves 'a deterritorialisation of temporal sequencing,' and therefore a deterritorialisation of straight time, through the 'paradoxical crossings' (Noble, 2012, p. 53) of various gender identities.

Intersexuality and the Construction of Gender

It is important to consider the social and medical perceptions of intersexuality, transsexuality and gender confirmation surgery when Heinlein wrote 'All You Zombies.' Heinlein explicitly refers to this cultural context in the story itself, when the Unmarried Mother compares his own transition with the transitions of Christine Jorgensen and Roberta Cowell, who were famous in Heinlein's generation (Ekins and King, 2006, p. 57) for having undergone gender confirmation surgery, then referred to as gender reassignment surgery: 'Look, ever hear of Christine Jorgenson? Or Roberta Cowell?' (AYZ, par. 28). However, in Jane's case, it truly is gender reassignment surgery, not gender confirmation surgery, in that she does not choose for the surgery to be performed upon her.

> 'But the surgeon was talking. "Tell me, uh—" He avoided my name. "did you ever think your glandular setup was odd?"
> 'I said, "Huh? Of course not. What are you driving at?"
> 'He hesitated. "I'll give you this in one dose, then a hypo to let you sleep off your jitters. You'll have 'em."
> '"Why?" I demanded.
> '"Ever hear of that Scottish physician who was female until she was thirty five? —then had surgery and became legally and medically a man? Got married. All okay."
> '"What's that got to do with me?"
> '"That's what I'm saying. You're a man."
> 'I tried to sit up. "What?" […] I started to cry.' (AYZ, par. 62-69)

The doctor callously informs Jane, post-surgery, that the deed has already been done, as Jane's female reproductive organs were irreparably damaged by childbirth and had to be removed, and, since she was intersex, converting her into a man was the only viable option. This preservation of the gender binary at the cost of the Jane's agency reflects the fact that, in Heinlein's era, the non-binary nature of intersexuality was shunned, and intersexuality was seen as an untenable medical condition that needed to be resolved by *making* the intersex person either male or female; no other, non-binary option or gender identity was permitted.

Even to this day, in most 'medical textbook[s], hermaphroditism [or intersexuality] is something that must be corrected' (Larbalestier, 2002, p. 92). Heinlein's portrayal of the tragic violation of Jane's forced surgery differs from other comparable New Wave depictions of intersexuality, like Theodore Sturgeon's *Venus Plus X* (1960) and Ursula K. Le Guin's *The Left Hand of Darkness* (1969), in which 'hermaphroditism or androgyny is transformed from a problem that must be surgically corrected into a possible solution to the problem of difference between men and women' (Larbalestier, 2002, p. 92). Heinlein's decision to instead depict the plight of the intersex individual in contemporary society, and the enforcement of the gender binary as cruel, calls the reader's attention to the heteronormative tyranny of the gender binary and its resulting oppression of non-binary people and identities.

> Intersex... is a core location... both made problematic and resolved by a binary and discrete conceptualisation of gender as a primary alignment, as a regime of living that guides medical practice and holds binary gender together... [A]pproaches to hermaphroditism repeatedly... use the phenomenon to reinforce the binary model, rather than to question it. (Karkazis, 2008, p. 14, p. 31)

This medical pathologisation of intersexuality directly results in Jane's forced gender change surgery. She is not given an option, because an option, as far as the doctor is concerned, does not exist; if she cannot biologically be a woman, then she must be a man. This pathologisation 'is based on the erroneous sex binary' (Inch, 2016, p. 193) and causes real damage to people, damage that is reflected in Heinlein's fictional depiction of intersexuality. The trauma of Jane's non-consensual surgery remains with the protagonist, who, now forced to live as a man, continues to write confessions from a woman's perspective and chooses the pseudonym 'of the 'Unmarried Mother,' indicating that the protagonist's internal gender identity has not entirely changed, even though the pronouns he uses to address himself have. Similarly, the Bartender, at the end of the story, still identifies as Jane and retains not only the physical scar of the C-section that delivered 'her' baby, but the mental and emotional memory of being a mother. Essentially, by the end of the story, the protagonist's gender identity is non-binary, because regardless of pronouns, the protagonist's *mind* remains unchanged and retains the same psychological continuity between different temporal and gendered states.

Gendering the Detective

Tonally, 'All You Zombies' has much in common with 1940s-1950s detective crime aesthetics. The noir genre is repeatedly referenced in the story via the rough talk of the characters, the grittiness of the bar setting, the discussion of tough city life, and the deployment of various terms generally reserved for noir fiction. Among these terms are 'hackie' (AYZ, par. 133), meaning cab driver, and 'sap' (AYZ, par. 7, 103), a leathery impact weapon often used by and against hard-boiled detectives like Raymond Chandler's archetypal detective, Philip Marlowe. Indeed, '[a] sap is seen or mentioned 29 times' (Escobar, 2018, ch. 10) in just a single Marlowe novel, *Farewell, My Lovely* (1940), and hence the term's presence in 'All You Zombies' is all the more conspicuous as a reference to detective noir. The name 'Jane,' too, is standard hard-boiled detective vernacular for 'woman' (Denton, 2016). These terms are clues to the mystery behind the story, not only the mystery of who the Bartender is, but the mystery of how the gender binary is set up and then dismantled through time travel.

The Bartender is introduced as a Marlowe-esque narrator; his language register neatly fits into the 'streetwise, tough-talking, and heavy-drinking' prototype of the hard-boiled noir protagonist (Aronson and Kimmel, 2004, p. 132). The Chandlerian hyper-masculinity of the hard-boiled detective (Abbott, 2003, p. 313) is an interesting tonal choice for Heinlein's initial characterisation of the Bartender, considering that the Bartender—who begins the story by using the markedly gruff, curt, hard-boiled language usually associated in noir fiction with undiluted masculinity—ends the story by calling himself a woman's name, 'Jane,' and reminiscing about his abdominal scar from a Caesarean section. This abruptly switches the narrative from the masculine language register of detective noir to the feminine language register of childbirth and motherhood.

> I undressed, and when I got down to the hide I looked at my belly. A Caesarean leaves a big scar... There isn't anybody but me—Jane... (AYZ, par. 156-162)

The feminine register is in operation in the above quote, since the 'female register... embodies the female role in our society' (Crosby and Nyquist, 1977, p. 314), including the role of motherhood. The C-section scar on the Bartender's body is an enduring physical reminder of 'his' internal femininity, of 'his' female past that can never be entirely erased, and must therefore be absorbed, resulting in a non-binary subjective experience that combines manhood with womanhood. If society perceives 'female speech [as] typically indirect, repetitious, and unclear while male speech is typically direct, clear, and precise' (Crosby and Nyquist, 1977, p. 314), then, by situating the hyper-masculine register of detective noir within the overarching indirectness and repetitiousness of time travel, the narrative feminises and sabotages that seeming masculinity, and blurs the border between male and female.

The construction of the Bartender's masculinity is crucial for its eventual deconstruction, inasmuch as the latter cannot take place without the former. Hard-boiled detective fiction hinges on the plot's central mystery that is simultaneously 'an investigation of the hero's masculinity as it is tested and proved through his solving of the case' (Aronson and Kimmel, 2004, p. 216), but the solving of the Bartender's case undermines his initial masculinity instead of reinforcing it. This is the mechanism upon which the deconstruction of the gender binary hinges within 'All You Zombies.' The use of detective noir aesthetics constructs and deconstructs the Bartender's masculinity; it initially tips the scale in favour of the 'male' half of the gender binary, tips it back towards femininity with the Unmarried Mother's flashback to Jane's experiences as a woman and mother, and finally, at the end of the story, strikes a precarious, porous, osmotic balance between the two genders that intermixes gender coding cues, disrupts the gendered binary construct, and alludes to the protagonist's non-binary gender identity.

> I'm so hairy now that I don't notice [the Cesarean scar] unless I look for it. (AYZ, par. 156)

The complexity of the time-travelling storyline, consisting of time paradoxes such as the Bartender's creation of himself, requires detective work from the reader. Just as the Bartender has to actively look for his scar, the reader has to actively look for clues. In hard-boiled detective fiction and in the noir films based on it, the reader/viewer is a co-creator who 'picks up cues, recalls information, anticipates what will follow, and generally participates in the creation of the [narrative which]… shapes particular expectations by summoning up curiosity, suspense, and surprise' (Bordwell and Thompson, 2008, p. 75). 'All You Zombies' borrows further from detective fiction by peppering the narrative with clues for the reader to pick up, such as when the jukebox in the Bartender's seedy, noir-ish bar 'blared out: "I'm My Own Grandpaw!" ' (AYZ, par. 116), hinting at the fact that the Bartender sired himself. The Bartender's repeated use of the possessive pronoun 'my' in referring to the Unmarried Mother as 'my boy' (AYZ, par. 2) and, most tellingly, 'my Unmarried Mother' (AYZ, par. 116), again implies that the Unmarried Mother is the Bartender's own mother, just as the Bartender is the Unmarried Mother's father. Another vital clue is the Bartender's fake wedding ring, which symbolises time travel, time paradoxes and the disruption of linear, binary time:

> 'It just looks like a wedding ring; I wear it to keep women off.' It is an antique I bought in 1985 from a fellow operative—he had fetched it from pre-Christian Crete. 'The Worm Ouroboros... the World Snake that eats its own tail, forever without end. A symbol of the Great Paradox.' (AYZ, par. 25)

The ring reveals to the reader that the Bartender is a time traveller, and not only that, but a time traveller caught in an endless repetition of his own personal life-cycle. When the Bartender claims that, 'A thing either is, or it isn't, now and forever amen' (AYZ, par. 145), it is, on its surface, a starkly binary statement about is-ness or is-*not*-ness, about the presence or absence of anything, including gender and sex. However, this binary statement is continuously and ironically interrogated by the Bartender's own actions, as he travels backwards and forwards in time, impregnates *and* gives birth to himself, and proves that his identity cannot be boiled down to as simple a binary matrix as male versus female, or here versus not here. Every time-state and gender-state always exists for the Bartender; there is no 'either is... or isn't' in the Bartender's own subjective experience. The Bartender experiences all the times he travels to as one long, seamless *now*; the dates change as he steps in and out of the time machine, but his personal, psychological continuity remains undisturbed. This continuity is the thread tying all the subtextual clues together.

The protagonist's psychological continuity, referred to by Heinlein scholar Mary Ellen Ryder as a 'character trace' (2003, p. 224), is built via 'cross-frame clues [that]

are encoded in nominal descriptions' and in varying
'context frames' (2003, p. 225). This encoding of context
frames is performed, within 'All You Zombies,' by the
subtle accretion of gendered cues, including those of the
detective noir genre, as just discussed. These context
frames share a 'co-referentiality' in that they continuously
refer to one another. All versions of the protagonist—the
Bartender, the Unmarried Mother, Jane, and the baby—
have their own seemingly independent (to begin with)
context frames, with each accorded a particular biological
sex and gender identity. The separate context frames are
created through the gender assignation of the characters;
part of the reader's ability to distinguish these apparently
different characters is that they have different genders *and*
bodies. Of course, the climax of the story is the reader's
'shock of discovering that all the characters are the same
person' (Ryder, 2003, p. 218). However, the efficacy
of this shock depends on the success of the narrative's
prior concealments, which borrows from the mystery
and thriller genres, especially from detective noir, in that
the reader must also do detective work by following the
protagonist's character trace through different context
frames. The reader does this by picking up 'cross-frame
clues,' i.e. clues created by the literary device of time
travel that allows crossing between frames. The reader
is invited, alongside the Unmarried Mother, to gather the
clues that put together the true identity of the protagonist,
an identity which includes the Unmarried Mother himself.

Thus, it is to be expected that the tone of the story is
also that of hard-boiled detective noir, borrowing, at the
beginning, from the hyper-masculine tonality of noir and

being deconstructed, by the end, to a borderline feminine gender-fluidity in which the protagonist refers to himself as 'Jane,' and ultimately drops the curt, stoic language of hard-boiled noir for the emotive one of femininity: 'There isn't anybody but me—Jane—here alone in the dark. I miss you dreadfully!' (AYZ, par. 161-162). The removal of the Bartender's mask of masculinity is as important to the queering of the text as the revelation that Jane is intersex.

Interestingly, this also draws a contrast between ignorance as straight/hyper-masculine and knowledge as queer/hypo-feminine. The reader's initial assumption that the Bartender is unequivocally masculine is progressively undermined as the language of masculinity is hijacked by the language of femininity, and the original assumption of the protagonist's cisgenderism is overtaken by the Unmarried Mother's confessions of intersexuality and womanhood. As the reader follows the 'cross-frame clues' of time travel and progresses through the narrative towards a more complete knowledge of the protagonist, the reader also transitions from straight time to queer time, in that the text (and the protagonist) is progressively queered, a queering facilitated by the protagonist confessing to being a man and a mother, being a father and Jane. The noir stereotype of the 'traumatized but tough' hero (Aronson and Kimmel, 2004, p. 216) is thoroughly dismantled by the fact that the protagonist's primary trauma in 'All You Zombies' is the *involuntary infliction of masculinity* through forced gender reassignment surgery. Masculinity is not a preferred state for the protagonist; to Jane, at least to begin with, it was an unwanted imposition.

Gendering Work

The hyper-masculinity of hard-boiled detective noir has a socioeconomic impetus. Considering that 'noir… is generally understood… as being largely about the acute sense of disempowerment men felt returning home from World War II to find that during the war women had left the domestic sphere and entered the workforce in unprecedented numbers' (Grant, 2011, p. 6), Heinlein's creation of noir-style masculinity in 'All You Zombies' depends heavily on the depiction of work. The concomitant creation of a seemingly opposing femininity depends on work, as well. Mendelsohn states that '[w]ork is for two purposes in Heinlein's construction of masculinity. It is there to develop the human being but it is also there to support a family (the second is rarely applied to women)' (2019, p. 418). The Unmarried Mother and Jane are both preoccupied with work, and though they are both the same person, their experience of work differs drastically pre- and post-transition, emblemising the stark differences between male and female gender roles, and the socioeconomic implications of the gender binary. Jane, who realises at a young age that she cannot depend on marriage to support herself because of her physical unattractiveness—she is 'horse-faced and buck-toothed, flat-chested and straight-haired' (AYZ, par. 32)—decides to go into sex work. If she volunteers for the respected role of a sex worker with the space corps, her unattractiveness won't matter:

> I [wouldn't] need looks; if they accepted me, they would
> fix my buck teeth, put a wave in my hair, teach me to walk

and dance and how to listen to a man pleasingly... They would even use plastic surgery if it would help... Best yet, they made sure you didn't get pregnant during your enlistment—and you were almost certain to marry at the end of your hitch. Same way today, *A.N.G.E.L.S.* marry spacers—they talk the language. (AYZ, 36-37)

Jane's only career choice as an orphaned girl of less-than-average looks hinges on the commodification of her body as a sex object, with the objectification going so far as to potentially result in cosmetic surgery to improve her attractiveness. In the eyes of society, Jane's body defines her completely. Her lack of perceived beauty influences her work prospects and earning potential for life. As a woman, Jane is not given the option of supporting a family without marrying first; she can only hope that by pursuing a career of sex work, she will eventually secure a husband to support her and her children, and grant her social respectability. But then, Jane is forced to undergo gender reassignment surgery and all her hopes are dashed:

I was no longer a woman... and I didn't know how to be a man... I don't mean learning how to dress, or not walking into the wrong rest room; I learned those in the hospital. But how could I live? What job could I get? Hell, I couldn't even drive a car. I didn't know a trade; I couldn't do manual labor—too much scar tissue, too tender. (AYZ, par. 93)

While the new, male version of Jane is initially lost, because 'he' grew up as a woman and was taught no useful skills, his new manhood permits him to pursue careers other than sex work. The Unmarried Mother, as a man, can find work as something else, even if it is not the most reliable source of income; he finds work as a 'fry cook, then... a public stenographer' (AYZ, par. 95). A man's looks do not restrict his working options as much; as the Unmarried Mother sarcastically asks, 'Who cares how a barkeep looks? Or a writer?' (AYZ, par. 34).

Ironically, what finally allows the Unmarried Mother to earn a stable income is writing about his erstwhile female experiences. As an unattractive woman, he struggled to find work, and his voice was not heard, but now, as a man, he makes his living by penning female narratives—a sly comment on how women's voices are often oppressed, erased and overtaken by men, who can profit off women's stories in a way that women themselves cannot.

This depiction of the gender binary through differences in work exposes the socioeconomic injustices of the binary system and provides a moral motivation for its dismantling. Through time travel, temporal disruption and gender change, Jane finally rises to the level of owning a bar and working as a time agent—a career far beyond what she had eventually envisioned. She is now the Bartender, who still bears Jane's C-section scar and carries Jane's memories; she is now a man that remembers being a woman, and thus occupies a genderfluid psychological space that defies the gender binary and liberates both her female and male selves from society's restrictions. As a time agent, the Bartender has moved beyond social expectations altogether; 'he' travels across time, never living in or contained by any particular epoch, engineering not only his own fate but the fates of others.

> Some agents con a subject into the net; I tell the truth and
> use that instant of utter astonishment to flip the switch.
> Which I did. (AYZ, par. 122)

Heinlein, too, does not 'con' the 'subject,' or the reader,
into his 'net'; he simply exposes the truth of who the
Bartender is and thereby 'flip[s] the switch' of gender, not
merely from female to male, as Jane's surgery did, but from
binary to non-binary.

Queering Reproduction

If 'temporal sequencing' is a 'horizon of social reproduction'
(Ahmed, 2006, p. 83), then 'All You Zombies' disrupts
that sequencing through a non-linear temporal loop. It
queers reproduction by converting the seemingly linear,
heterosexual act of conception and birth into a circular,
non-linear, queer act, since both parties involved in the
biological conception of themselves have been male, female
and intersex at various points in their non-linear timeline,
and their offspring will also become themselves, and will
eventually be male, female and intersex.

Indeed, because it is non-linear and embodied in the
ever-changing gendered space of the protagonist's body, the
narrative arc is not so much a time*line* as it is a time-space,
or, as Bakhtin would call it, a 'chronotope' (Bakhtin, 1981,
p. 84). Moreover, it is a queer chronotope because it exists
in 'queer time,' which Halberstam defines as 'a term for
those specific models of temporality that emerge… once one
leaves the temporal frames of bourgeois reproduction and
family, longevity, risk/safety, and inheritance' (Halberstam,

2005, p. 6). In 'All You Zombies,' Heinlein departs from the temporal frames of bourgeois reproduction, i.e. the heteronormative concept of the nuclear family consisting of father, mother and child. This creates a queer inheritance that differs from the linear, parent-to-child progression of straight inheritance by writing a non-binary, variously gendered character that is both their own parent *and* their own child, in a never-ending, non-linear loop. The longevity that results for the protagonist is a sort of queer immortality, which entails the self-seduction and self-conception of doppelgängers that are all variously intersex, male, female, and genderqueer.

Doctoring Gender, Paradoctoring Time

In 'All You Zombies,' the default gender binary, as represented by the apparently cisgender male protagonist at the very start of the story, is progressively deconstructed by the deconstruction of the protagonist himself/herself/themselves. Each spatiotemporal deconstruction unpacks another, like a set of nested Russian dolls. The seemingly male 'Bartender' is revealed to be the 'Unmarried Mother,' who is revealed to have been 'Jane,' an intersex woman forced via surgery to become a biological man, who is then revealed to have been the man who impregnated her, and who is finally revealed to be the child born of that union, a child that grows up to be the Bartender. This dizzying conglomeration of time loops is a form of temporal montage, and montage, according to Derrida, is 'one of the most effective strategies in putting into question [...] all the illusions of representation' (1981, p. 26). The key illusion of representation in this short story is the illusion of binary gender and its attendant illusion of gender-as-being—or, to be more exact, of the straight linearity of *gender defining being* (i.e. gender preexisting being), rather than the queer non-linearity of *being defining gender* (i.e. being preexisting, coexisting with *and* post-existing gender, implying that gender can be endlessly revisioned through any of these temporal entry-points). The plot is, in essence, a literary Möbius strip in which free will and the Nietzschean eternal recurrence of 'a circular... self-perpetuating plot' (Wittenberg, 2013, p. 217) cohabitate within the protagonist, granting that protagonist agency while also robbing them of it.

The chronotope of the time-travelling gendered body is here a discursive, recursive self-creation that simultaneously strengthens and hijacks the protagonist's agency, for while the initial, involuntary gender reassignment surgery performed on the protagonist lacks agency, the actions leading to that surgery are within the protagonist's purview and are a direct result of his/her/their actions. And yet, she/he/they must repeat those actions *ad infinitum* or risk destroying themselves; the protagonist has to go back in time and conceive themselves as both man and woman, or risk never having been born at all. This temporal paradox can be read either as a genderqueer affirmation that the non-binary nature of the protagonist is crucial to the protagonist's survival and cannot be destroyed or erased even by surgery, or as a condemnation of gender alterity in which being genderqueer is in itself punishable, a deformity requiring medical correction, an extension of the depravities of incest that leads to a doomed karmic cycle from which the protagonist can never escape.

This doubling of morality is a byproduct of the doubling

of the protagonist's psyche, a past/present, male/female 'doubling of consciousness where both—indeed, all sides of consciousness—exist in a profound complex relative to time and to what haunts temporal modernities as one of the ingredients in subject formation' (Noble, 2012, p. 53). If the subject being formed is the protagonist, then the doubling of the protagonist's consciousness exists in a 'profound complex' of time and gender, an in-flux chronotope that constantly revises and reinvents itself. Unlike many time travel stories, which are non-deterministic and centre on the free will of the characters to alter time and edit history, 'All You Zombies' posits a deterministic, even fatalistic temporal model that, while acknowledging and even at times seeming to celebrate non-heteronormativity, nevertheless exposes that the linearity of straight time inevitably robs the genderqueer person of their agency, be it through surgery or enforced social conformity. A non-binary genderqueer identity can, in that sense, only survive in queer time, which is non-linear and is concurrently experienced as past, present *and* future, without any divisions or demarcations. It is only in the absence of the divisions and linear orderedness of heteronormativity that the fullness of a genderqueer identity can endure and become recognisable to its owner, as it is to the Bartender, who exists outside of straight time and can engineer that time through a time machine. The Bartender, who is the narrator-protagonist, lives in queer time, where all temporal states coexist; that is what gives him his temporal omniscience and his compounded, aggregated knowledge of himself as genderqueer. Even so, his actions are still fated, despite being freely chosen, and this conflict between 'free will and fatalism' is central to many time travel stories (Nahin, 1998, p. 49). 'All You Zombies' is yet another example of the 'predestination paradox' (Rooney, 2017, p. 129), in which a character cannot escape their fate despite exercising free will, a paradox that the Bartender nonetheless believes can be 'paradoctored' (AYZ, par. 152).

Thus, while it questions the value and validity of heteronormativity, Heinlein's short story also questions the freedom of non-heteronormativity, especially in a world that enforces heteronormativity regardless of the individual's identity, such as when surgery forces a man's body onto the intersex protagonist despite their initially identifying as a woman. This fatalism can be read in two ways: as a punishment of queerness, or as a resistance against straight time. The first reading is problematic in that it reinforces the social injustices already inherent in the gender binary, injustices that often condemn intersex people to the same non-consensual surgery that the protagonist of 'All You Zombies' undergoes. The second, more optimistic reading, which can be seen as an application of Sedgwick's 'reparative reading' (Edwards, 2008, p. 111), equalises all forms and presentations of gender by making them all equally subject to fate. If, as in the Oedipus myth, the agency of the protagonist still results in them making choices that lead to an unavoidable fate, then this is evidence of the protagonist's *hamartia*, or fatal flaw, which is not due to any 'specific sin attaching to [them] as an individual, but the universally human one of blindly following the light of one's own intellect,' a blindness that culminates in what is 'the essence of tragedy: suffering without moral guilt' (Van Braam, 1912, pp. 271-272).

Consequently, through reparative reading, the fate of the

Bartender is not a punishment for his/her/their queerness, but a more generalised punishment for the human hubris of seeking to control and alter time. There is no 'moral guilt' involved in this reading, no punishment of perceived perversion. The story is also not entirely a tragedy, for the Bartender's actions clearly lead to his/her/their self-preservation, even if it is a somewhat lost, fractured existence, in which the now-male protagonist looks down at the scar from the Caesarean section performed on him when he gave birth to himself, and plaintively asks: 'I know where I came from—but where did all you zombies come from?' (AYZ, par. 158). The use of the word 'zombies' is a vital clue, not only because it is a part of the story's title and is therefore a significant tell as to authorial intention, but because it exposes the protagonist's true sentiments regarding all his different synecdochic selves. Beloved as they are to him, as his erstwhile lovers, parents and child, they are also 'zombies' to him, unnatural creatures that cannot die, even if they (and he) wish to. Instead of being liberated by death, these zombies can only march mindlessly upon their circular causal path, freely choosing to imprison themselves, oxymoronic and ironic though that statement may be. While the Bartender is surviving, his own survival distresses him, because it is a 'weird undeath' that never quite reaches 'the subject's own fulfilled death wish' (Wittenberg, 2013, p. 209). Eternity cycles on, and the Bartender with it, following the steps of the same intricate dance of cause and effect over and over again. While the Bartender does contemplate retiring from his job as a time agent at the end of the story—and therefore leaving this unending cycle—he is still locked in its loop within the spatiotemporal narrative of the story.

As the narratologist Rimmon-Kenan says, '[c]omplete repetition, then, is death or—if one prefers—eternity,' because 'some repetitions… serve the pleasure principle, while others seem to manifest a death instinct' (1980, pp. 154-155). According to Rimmon-Kenan, 'the distinguishing feature' between these two types of repetition is that the former is a 'successful, constructive, ultimately pleasurable repetition,' wherein the acteur 'gains mastery over the disagreeable experience,' whereas the latter is the acteur's submission to and subjugation by 'over-sameness' and existential despair (1980, p. 154). The protagonist of 'All You Zombies' is forever poised in a delicate balance between those two states, between mastery and subjugation, between ecstasy and despair; after all, 'Jane' and the 'Unmarried Mother,' both the same person, experience the ecstasy of romantic and sexual union with each other, only to be forcefully parted from one another and from their child, who in turn grows up to suffer from the ennui brought on by connecting to and detaching from the self again and again. The Bartender is both the maker of his fate, and the non-triumphant victim-master of fate's inexorable, numbing repetition. When the Bartender watches his younger self, the Unmarried Mother, kissing his female self, Jane, for the umpteenth time, he is no longer moved by it. Instead, the scene is now rote to him and removed from him, a temporally induced dissociation, and all he can think of, instead of recalling the intensity of the passion he/she/ they had experienced, is that the kiss is taking too long. In this, the Bartender wavers between the desensitising 'over-sameness' of repetition and his 'successful, constructive' if not 'pleasurable' control of it.

'That's what I'm saying. You're a man.'
I tried to sit up. 'What?' [...] I started to cry. 'What about
my baby?' (AYZ, par. 68-69)

Furthermore, as the above quote illustrates, not every
'disagreeable experience' of the protagonist's is mastered.
That Jane, the female version of the protagonist before her
forced sex change surgery, had no control over her own
physical transformation, remains a traumatic memory for
the Unmarried Mother, who confesses, 'I was no longer
a woman... and I didn't know how to be a man' (AYZ,
par. 91). This does indeed reflect the experiences of many
intersex people, who are forced at a very young age to
undergo cosmetic and/or genital reconstruction surgery
without their consultation, 'unnecessary surgeries that are
non-consensual and are irreversible, and that can have so
many consequences... [M]ost of the surgeries are based
on fear of non-binary bodies' ('I'm Intersex,' par. 4).
While Jane's surgery is medically unavoidable within the
framework of the story, her distress at being biologically
and sexually altered without her consent is unfortunately
a familiar intersex narrative, and one that often 'requires
taking back an identity which has been made illegitimate by
culture... and stolen through surgery' (Feinberg, 1996, p.
139). In 'All You Zombies,' the Bartender—who is also the
Unmarried Mother and Jane—can only take back his/her/
their identity through temporal shifts and rifts, and although
they eventually become comfortable in a male body as
well, the inherent queerness of the protagonist remains. In
fact, as stated before, Jane's surgery represents 'the history
of understandings of and approaches to hermaphroditism

[that] repeatedly... use the phenomenon to reinforce the binary model, rather than to question it' (Karkazis, 2008, p. 31). The surgery has a similarly stultifying effect on the narrative, temporarily reinforcing the gender binary. While heterosexuality momentarily prevails, especially when the newly minted male version of Jane finds himself 'staring down nurses' necklines' (AYZ, par. 85), he goes on to maintain the queerness of the narrative by falling in love with Jane, his own previous self.

Heinlein's choice of an intersex protagonist is hence a deliberate queering of the text, particularly since intersexuality itself confronts and disrupts the heteronormative, he/she gender binary. While the forced surgical removal of the gender ambiguity inherent in Jane can be seen as an erasure of her queerness, Heinlein's depiction of the procedure is sympathetic towards Jane, to whom that procedure is a shocking violation, a personal tragedy that haunts her even when she becomes the Unmarried Mother and, decades later, the Bartender. In 'effacing physiological sexual ambiguity,' the surgery 'upholds the sex and gender binary by making a delineation between the sexes clear, even if it is technologically constructed' (Preves, 2005, p. 57). However, as a narratological event, Jane's surgery arouses the sympathy of the reader *in favour* of that ambiguity, not against it. It is important to note that the 'fear of non-binary bodies' ('I'm Intersex,' par. 4) that leads to many such non-consensual surgeries among real intersex people is, at its base, not only a fear of the violation of the gender binary, but also a fear of alternate sexual identities. After all, 'if physiological sex is ambiguous, discussion of sexual orientation seems impossible because traditional understandings of sexual orientation are rooted in a binary understanding of sex' (Preves, 2005, p. 58). Essentially, the heteronormative *status quo* is threatened both by non-binary gender *and* its implication that sexual identities are not clearly identifiable and divisible, for if binary gender does not exist, then there is nothing to separate heterosexuality from homosexuality, or from any other sexuality. Heterosexuality cannot, then, be privileged; indeed, it cannot even survive. This existential panic is at the root of forced medical surgeries performed on intersex people, because '[s]exual ambiguity problematises this binary thinking' (Preves, 2005, p. 58). Enforcing the gender binary in literal, physical terms is as much a broader social act of oppression and erasure of non-heteronormativity as it is a medical act that affects an individual.

In choosing to make his protagonist intersex and in choosing to depict the cruelty of the policing of the intersex body, Heinlein raises the question of whether the gender binary need be enforced in such an inhumane manner, particularly when that enforcement is bound to be a failure, anyway. Jane might have been surgically altered and forced to live as a man, but the Bartender, many years later, still bears the scar of the Caesarian section once performed upon 'him,' and still retains all the memories and emotions that belonged to 'his' previous female self. Similarly, the Unmarried Mother continues to write under that pseudonym because 'he' still remembers the grief of losing 'her' child, and of being abandoned by 'her' lover. The protagonist's non-binary identity *remains non-binary* regardless of their body being forcefully changed, for the heart and the mind are not so easily altered. In Heinlein's story, queerness persists, survives and overcomes its persecution; its erasure by society does not succeed. If '[q]ueer temporalities… are points of resistance to this temporal order that, in turn, propose other possibilities for living in relation to indeterminately past, present, and future others' (Freeman, 2010, p. xxii), then Jane's surgery and post-surgery resistance to the gender binary is not so much a sympathetic victimisation of her, intended merely to evoke pity, but a powerful point of resistance against heteronormativity, against the 'temporal order' of straight time. The 'indeterminately past, present and future' versions of the protagonist that are Jane, the Unmarried Mother and the Bartender are in essence a fusion, reclamation and restoration of the protagonist's non-binary gender identity. In 'All You Zombies,' queer time is never quite vanquished by straight time; non-heteronormativity is never vanquished by heteronormativity, despite society's attempts to make it so.

The Longing of Narcissus

Another instance of textual queering is when the Bartender remarks to his younger self, who has just seduced and impregnated their female self: '[Y]ou can't resist seducing yourself' (AYZ, par. 137). The genderqueer multiplicity of variously gendered selves renders the sexual intercourse that occurs between the Unmarried Mother and Jane homoerotic/autoerotic, because the protagonist is attracted to themselves. Even if the impregnation is a product of seemingly heterosexual sex, both protagonists are, in effect, intersex and genderqueer. Just as the myth of Narcissus is necessarily queer because Narcissus is enraptured by himself, i.e. by a person of the same sex, so is the protagonist of 'All You Zombies' queer because he/she/they have been in love with—and, as per the story's ending, *remain* in love with—a past male self and a past female self, indicating an innate bisexuality or pansexuality. Bisexuality is a non-binary sexuality, as is evidenced by the following quote from a bisexual magazine:

> Bisexuality is a whole, fluid identity. Don't assume that bisexuality is binary or duogamous in nature: that we must have 'two' sides or that we MUST be involved simultaneously with both genders to be fulfilled human beings. In fact, don't assume that there are only two genders. Do not mistake our fluidity for confusion, irresponsibility, or an inability to commit. Do not equate promiscuity, infidelity, or unsafe sexual behavior with bisexuality. These are human traits that cross ALL sexual orientations. Nothing should be assumed about anyone's sexuality—including your own. (Garber, 1995, p. 56)

Of course, in 'All You Zombies,' the bisexual desire present in the text is directed by the protagonist towards the protagonist's own male and female selves, which implies a degree of self-eroticisation. Yet the parallels with Narcissus do not end there. A queer reading of Narcissus must account not only for the figure's innate homoeroticism, but for 'the figure who *rejects...* the very notion of a stable gender,' and in so doing rejects 'not only the dictate to desire... a socially prescribed and approved other... but also the drive to stabilise a range of binarisms upon which gender in Western culture is founded' (Bruhm, 2001, p. 15). The protagonist of 'All You Zombies' typifies this phenomenon, by desiring the self instead of a socially prescribed other, and by rejecting the illusory stability of the gender binary by occupying a variety of differently gendered bodies and subscribing to a variety of differently gendered identities. Like Whitman, the protagonist contains multitudes. The dialogue within the story is also narcissistic in that virtually all the dialogue is self-directed as the protagonist converses with himself/herself/themselves, in what is an infinite echoing of voices within the temporal echo chamber of the narrative. Like the myth of Narcissus, the myth of Echo is also 'a myth that circles around same-sex erotic desire' and is therefore 'a queerly disruptive paradigm' (Bruhm, 2001, p. 13). The autoeroticism inherent in the protagonist's echoing of themselves renders the narrative of 'All You Zombies' queer, as does the fact that the protagonist is effectively a series of self-reflecting mirrors. Reflection as self-knowledge is central to the development of human identity; the Lacanian 'mirror stage' is what allows a human being to experience themselves as a 'unified totality,' before which they can only perceive themselves as 'something disjointed' (Dor, 2004, p. 95). The Bartender, the Unmarried Mother and Jane are all perpetually undergoing a mirror stage of meeting and identifying with their reflections. As Truman Capote, himself a queer author, says of mirrors:

> They can romanticise us so, mirrors, and that is their secret: what a subtle torture it would be to destroy all the mirrors in the world: where then could we look for reassurance of our identities? I tell you, my dear, Narcissus was no egotist... he was merely another of us who, in our unshatterable isolation, recognised, on seeing his reflection, the one beautiful comrade, the only inseparable love... (Capote, 1963, ch. 8, par. 5)

At the very end of the story, the Bartender, who still also identifies as Jane, expresses a yearning for his/her/their other selves, a profound loneliness at being without their mirrors: 'You aren't really there at all. There isn't anybody but me—Jane—here alone in the dark. I miss you dreadfully!' (AYZ, par. 161-162). Time travel, for the Bartender/Unmarried Mother/Jane, has become their only means of completing themselves and fusing with themselves, their only balm to soothe the ache of being a fractured entity. They suffer from the 'subtle torture' of being an image that is incomplete without its reflection, a mirror that is desolate without anything to reflect. This Narcissus-like longing for the self does not require the existence of an other, and, as stated above, queers the narrative by deconstructing the need for binary pairs (self/other, male/female, past/future) altogether. The protagonist can be read as queer precisely because they reject any desire that is based on the dichotomy of self and other; they have no need for an other, since only the self can be their 'one beautiful comrade,' their 'only inseparable love,' and union with that self is the only sense of wholeness available to them through the repeated disruptions of time.

Conclusion

Is the deconstruction of binary gender complete in 'All You Zombies'? No, but for a text written when it was—in the 1950s—it is nonetheless progressive in its handling of gender identity. As Alex Iantaffi says in their essay in *Genderqueer and Non-Binary Genders*, the 'inclusion of non-binary genders is likely to look somewhat different than it might have been, because of our different temporal location' (2017, p. 293). As much as the Bartender is a time traveller, so are we, and our perception of Heinlein's story and its attempt at an 'inclusion of non-binary genders' differs from what our perception of the same story may have been in Heinlein's own time, when it was considerably more shocking. While 'All You Zombies' does not offer as open a view of gender as we might expect from a contemporary author of speculative fiction—such as Everett Maroon, who is studied in the next chapter—it nonetheless draws the reader into a consideration of what it means to be fundamentally human, regardless of the shape of one's body or the expectations of heteronormative gender roles that are placed upon it.

References

Aronson, A. and Kimmel, M. (2004) *Men and Masculinities: A Social, Cultural, and Historical Encyclopedia, Volume I: A–J.* Santa Barbara: ABC Clio.

Abbott, M.E. (2003) 'Nothing You Can't Fix: Screening Marlowe's Masculinity,' *Studies in the Novel*, 35(3), pp. 305-324.

Ahmed, S. (2006). *Queer Phenomenology: Orientations, Objects, Others*. Durham: Duke University Press.

Bakhtin, M. (1981) *The Dialogic Imagination.* Austin: Texas University Press.

Bordwell, D. and Thompson, K. (2008) *Film Art: An Introduction.* New York: McGraw-Hill.

Bruhm, S. (2001) *Reflecting Narcissus: A Queer Aesthetic.* Minneapolis: Minnesota University Press.

Capote, T. (1963) *Other Voices, Other Rooms*. New York: Signet.

Chandler, R. (1940) *Farewell, My Lovely*. New York: Alfred A. Knopf.

Crosby, F. and Nyquist, L. (1977) 'The Female Register: An Empirical Study of Lakoff's Hypotheses,' *Language in Society*, 6(3), pp. 313-322.

Denton, W. (2016) 'Twists, Slugs and Roscoes: A Glossary of Hardboiled Slang.' Miskatonic University Press, 25 May [online]. Available at: <https://www.miskatonic.org/slang.html> (Accessed 25 February 2020).

Derrida, J. (1981) *Positions*. Translated by A. Bass. Chicago: University of Chicago.

Dor, J. (2004) *Introduction to the Reading of Lacan: The Unconscious Structured Like a Language*. New York: Other Press.

Edwards, J. (2008) *Eve Kosofsky Sedgwick*. New York: Routledge.

Ekins, R. and King, D. (2006) *The Transgender Phenomenon*. Thousand Oaks: Sage Publications.

Enke, A.F. (2012) 'Introduction' in Enke, A.F. (ed.) *Transfeminist Perspectives: In and Beyond Transgender and Gender Studies*. Philadelphia: Temple University Press, pp. 1-15.

Escobar, R. (2018) *Saps, Blackjacks and Slungshots: A History of Forgotten Weapons*. Columbus: Gatekeeper Press.

Feinberg, L. (1996) *Transgender Warriors*. Boston: Beacon Press.

Freeman, E. (2010) *Time Binds: Queer Temporalities, Queer Histories*. Durham: Duke University Press.

Garber, M. (1995) *Vice Versa: Bisexuality and the Eroticism of Everyday Life*. New York: Simon & Schuster.

Grant, B.K. (2011) *Shadows of Doubt: Negotiations of Masculinity in American Genre Films*. Detroit: Wayne State University Press.

Halberstam, J. (2005) *In a Queer Time and Space*. New York: New York University Press.

Heinlein, R.A. (2018) 'All You Zombies.' *GitHub* [online]. Available at: <https://gist.github.com/defunkt/759182/ad44c6135d168ae54503a281bb7e1a24c6c2ea0c> (Accessed 25 February 2020).
---. (1959) 'By His Bootstraps.' *The Menace from Earth*. New York: Gnome Press.
---. (1953) 'Elsewhen.' *Assignment in Eternity*. Pennsylvania: Fantasy Press.
---. (1964) *Farnham's Freehold*. New York: G.P. Putnam.
---. (2003) *For Us, the Living: A Comedy of Customs*. New York: Scribner.
---. (1982) *Friday*. New York: Holt, Rinehart and Winston.
---. (1989) *Grumbles From the Grave*. New York: Ballantine Books.
---. (1970) *I Will Fear No Evil*. New York: G.P. Putnam's Sons.

---. (1961) *Stranger in a Strange Land*. New York: G.P. Putnam's Sons.

---. (1985) *The Cat Who Walks Through Walls*. New York: Putnam Publishing Group.

---. (1957) *The Door into Summer*. New York: Doubleday.

---. (1980) *The Number of the Beast*. New York: Fawcett.

---. (1973) *Time Enough for Love*. New York: G.P. Putnam.

---. (1987) *To Sail Beyond the Sunset*. New York: G.P. Putnam's Sons.

Holmes, M. (2008) *Intersex: A Perilous Difference*. Pennsylvania: Susquehanna University Press.

'I'm Intersex, And It's Way More Common Than You Think.' (2017) *Teen Vogue*, 2 July [online]. Available at: <https://www.teenvogue.com/story/intersex-video-periods-genital-mutilation-surgery-identity> (Accessed 25 February 2020).

Iantaffi, A. (2017) 'Future Directions' in Barker, M., Bouman, W.P. and Richards, C. (eds.) *Genderqueer and Non-Binary Genders*. London: Palgrave Macmillan, pp. 283-296.

Inch, E. (2016) 'Changing Minds: The Psycho-Pathologisation of Trans People,' *International Journal of Mental Health*, 45(3), pp. 193-204.

Karkazis, K. (2008) *Fixing Sex: Intersex, Medical Authority, and Lived Experience*. Durham: Duke University Press.

Larbalestier, J. (2002) *The Battle of the Sexes in Science Fiction.* Middletown: Wesleyan University Press.

Mendelsohn, F. (2019) *The Pleasant Profession of Robert A. Heinlein.* London: Unbound Publishing.

Nahin, P.J. (1998) *Time Machines: Time Travel in Physics, Metaphysics, and Science Fiction*. New Hampshire: New Hampshire University Press.

Noble, B. (2012) 'Trans. Panic. Some Thoughts Toward a Theory of Feminist Fundamentalism' in Enke, A.F. (ed.) *Transfeminist Perspectives:*

In and Beyond Transgender and Gender Studies. Philadelphia: Temple University Press, pp. 45-59.

Muñoz, J.E. (2009) *Cruising Utopia: The Then and There of Queer Futurity*. New York: New York University Press.

Preves, S.E. (2005) *Intersex and Identity: The Contested Self*. New Brunswick: Rutgers University Press.

Rimmon-Kenan, S. (1980) 'The Paradoxical Status of Repetition,' *Poetics Today*, 1(4), pp. 151-159.

Rochelle, W. (1999) 'Dual Attractions: The Rhetoric of Bisexuality in Robert A. Heinlein's Fiction,' *Foundation*, 76, pp. 48-62.

Rooney, A. (2017) *The History of Philosophy.* Buffalo: Rosen Publishing Group.

Ryder, M.E. (2003) 'I met myself coming and going: co(?)-referential noun phrases and point of view in time travel stories,' *Language and Literature*, 12(3), pp. 213-232.

Van Braam, P. (1912) 'Aristotle's Use of Ἁμαρτία,' *The Classical Quarterly*, 6(4), pp. 266-272.

Wittenberg, D. (2013) *Time Travel: The Popular Philosophy of Narrative*. New York: Fordham University Press.

CHAPTER THREE

Transing Time in Everett Maroon's
The Unintentional Time Traveler

> Why must the rupture of transgender so often be tamed
> into the temporal narrative of belated discovery, when we
> could imbue it with all the strength and inexplicability of
> the untimely?
> — Lucas Crawford, Transgender Architectonics.

Introduction

The Unintentional Time Traveler is a Young Adult novel
of speculative fiction by the transgender author Everett
Maroon. It features a protagonist who not only travels
between times, but between genders. Like the protagonist of
his novel, Maroon, too, is an epileptic, and his experiences
of epilepsy inform the novel (Maroon quoted in Kuiken,
2014, par. 7).

The protagonist of *The Unintentional Time Traveler*
is Jack, an initially cisgender-identifying teenage boy,
who undergoes medical treatment for epilepsy and, mid-
treatment, finds himself unexpectedly travelling back
to Prohibition-era America and into the body of a girl
named Jacqueline. In that violent period, Jack/Jacqueline

then falls in love with a young man named Lucas, and becomes committed to saving Lucas's life by changing history. By the end of the novel, the protagonist identifies firmly as Jacqueline and as a woman, and the character's transformation from male to female—both externally and internally—follows a transgender narrative in which Jack begins to doubt 'his' assigned-at-birth masculinity, ceases to identify with it, and slowly comes to identify as Jacqueline.

Sociotemporality

Maroon's novel interrogates the rigidity of gender roles by using time travel as a means of letting the protagonist exist not only outside the past and the future but outside of the gender binary altogether, thereby raising the question of how much of a role sociotemporal determinism plays in our gender identities. Before proceeding with my analysis of the text, I must explain what sociotemporality is.

'Sociotemporality' is the temporality of social ordering and conditioning, such that 'the sociotemporal order […] regulates the lives of *social* entities,' and, 'even though sociotemporal order is based, to a large extent, on purely arbitrary social convention, it is nevertheless perceived by people as given, inevitable, and unalterable' (Zerubavel, 1985, p. xii, p. 42). For example, if one is to take the Bible as a socially relevant text, especially in Western countries where Christianity is the most populous religion, then the Biblical depiction of Eve being formed from Adam's rib is a form of sociotemporal ordering—that is, it implies (and prescribes) Adam's superiority to Eve, and man's superiority to woman, based on the chronological order of their creation. This privileging acts not only as a narrativisation of sociotemporal ordering but also as the main bolstering force maintaining the gender binary itself. If all social dialogue is 'dual' and all 'social realities are […] dialogically constructed' (Markova, 2003, p. 15), then the establishing of binaries is essential to all social dialogue, be it progressive or, as in the case of the gender binary, oppressive. Only empathic dialogue that is an 'attunement to the attunement of the other' (Rommetveit, 1992, p. 23) is an antidote to dialogue based on an oppressive, alienating duality. *The Unintentional Time Traveler*, as we will see in this chapter, establishes an empathic, reparative dialogue between heteronormative/queer and cisgender/transgender, a dialogue that occurs through the transing of time.

I must also note that sociotemporality is a biological and scientifically observed phenomenon. In the human brain, '[t]emporal and social processing are intricately linked'; there is an observable interchange in image modelling between the part of the brain responsible for 'time perception' and 'social signals and social context,' which leads to a 'temporal […] organization of interactional behaviours both within and between individuals' (Meck, Schirmer and Penney, 2016, p. 760). This biological phenomenon is vital in understanding why the temporal organisation (or rather, disorganisation) of *The Unintentional Time Traveler* instigates within the protagonist a reordering of gender, which is a social behaviour, a social signal and a social context all at once. Time and gender are inextricably linked, as is evidenced by Jack/Jacqueline changing gender and time simultaneously; even neurologically, a change in time entails a change in gender processing and vice-versa.

In accompanying the protagonist through their temporally-induced gender transformations, the reader is invited to process gender differently, as well.

The time-traveler in *The Unintentional Time Traveler* journeys not between fictional times but between real, existing social histories such as Prohibition-era America and the first wave of the AIDS epidemic. In such reality-inspired time travel literature, the disruption of temporal order is inevitably also a disruption of social order, because 'narrative structure is a form of sociotemporal order and […] temporal referencing has important implications for […] conceptualizations of the world' (Squiers, 2014, p. 56). The temporal referencing and cross-referencing of multiple historical periods *and* multiple gendered narratives within Maroon's novel causes its protagonist to re-conceptualise widely accepted notions of gender identity and sexuality, and urges the reader to do the same.

As the protagonist journeys back and forth between contemporary America and Prohibition-era America and between the 'male' and 'female' sexes, the novel utilises these temporal environments' differing attitudes to gender and sexuality in a manner that provokes readers to think about what qualifies as progressive, and whether further potentialities exist for progressiveness in the future, if the present we live in is so much more progressive than its past. For example, Jack/Jacqueline is horrified by the lack of women's rights in the past that s/he travels to, and thus, upon returning to modernity, is more aware of the gender inequalities that still exist. Time travel reframes contemporary social issues in other historical contexts, driving the text's interrogation of cultural norms such as misogyny and heteronormativity.

An evolving sociotemporality also prompts revisionings of gender identity within the protagonist. The disordering of subjective linear time through time travel causes a concurrent disordering of the protagonist's own internal gender narrative, i.e. the story of their own gender development as they tell it to themselves. In the quotes below, for instance, Jack/Jacqueline occupies an overlapping psychological and sociotemporal space between genders, where they no longer identify entirely as Jack but do not yet completely identify as Jacqueline, either:

> At least he'd given me some space to cry. I didn't want to be in someone else's body, after months readjusting to mine. But I did, too. I wasn't sure what any of this made me [...] I was drawn to Lucas but I also worried that what we were doing was wrong. (TUTT, p. 155)[1]

> All the time in Jacqueline's life expressing emotions, experiencing things from her perspective, now this body felt foreign to me. *Who is Jack? What am I about?* (TUTT, p. 234)

Jack's/Jacqueline's realisation that one's gender need not be what is assigned to one at birth, and need not be exclusively male or female at all times, is a direct consequence of the sociotemporal reordering brought on by time travel, a literary device that, in this novel, metaphorises the transgender search for self. While initially distressing

---

1. For brevity, all in-text citations of *The Unintentional Time Traveler* will follow this abbreviated format.

because of the mismatch between internal gender identity and external biological sex, this search nonetheless repossesses and reclaims the gender binary from the jaws of heteronormativity. *The Unintentional Time Traveler* grants its protagonist re-entry into the binary system of gender by exercising free will. As the novel progresses, Jack, now Jacqueline, gains control of her time-traveling and her physical transformations. She reclaims her agency from an artificially imposed gender binary by instead choosing to participate in that gender binary of her own volition and as it suits her, entering into it and exiting from it as she wishes. Jacqueline then discovers that choosing to live as a particular gender is starkly different to having that gender imposed upon her by society. This queers the gender and sex binary in that it becomes an option instead of compulsory; the character can live outside of time and gender but can also enter into certain times and bodies at will, due to having mastered time travel by the novel's conclusion. Jacqueline's overarching, time-travelling transition from the male to the female sex and from the male to the female gender is a triumphant transgender parable, because, by the end of the novel, Jacqueline actively chooses to transition and fulfills her transgender agency.

That said, since Jack/Jacqueline largely switches between two gender settings, the gender binary is not completely deconstructed. Some of the questions regarding Jack's/ Jacqueline's gender identity are left unexplored by the end of the novel. However, perhaps this, too, is an authentic aspect of the genderqueer existence; gender identity is never 'complete' and, even after becoming certain of one's own gender identity, there are always questions about oneself that remain unexplored at any particular point in time. After all, '[a]n authentic self cannot be explained in non-temporal terms, as if there exists a static, finished, immutable entity, 'self' (Simmonds, 2012, p. 45). The 'authentic self' of the genderqueer and/or transgender individual can only be explored through temporality—particularly sociotemporality, as defined earlier in this chapter—but by this very token, is always incomplete, because any temporality is not static or finite. Temporality is always in flux, a continuous becoming, and none of us, whether we believe in linear or non-linear time, can say that we stand at the very end of time, beyond which no events and evolutions can occur.

> A systemic and intersectional framework of gender(s) entails a dynamic understanding of identities as fluid depending on special and temporal locations. Someone might express their non-binary identity more in one context, than another, depending on safety, opportunity, or simply desire. (Iantaffi, 2017, pp. 288-289)

Jack/Jacqueline's shifting pronouns, internal identifications and external manifestations represent this very fluidity, as well as the queer agency of having control over one's own gender expression and performing one's non-binary identity differently 'depending on special and temporal locations'—in Jack/Jacqueline's case, literal temporal locations that fluctuate as a result of time travel. This genderfluidity, as it is present within the novel, 'starts to dismantle several of the structures we have artificially created, in White Western minority cultures, around the gender binary' (Iantaffi, 2017, p. 289).

Crucially, *The Unintentional Time Traveler* also has an openly avowed trans man as an author, who has written a personal memoir about his experiences titled, *Bumbling Into Body Hair: Tales of an Accident-Prone Transsexual* (Maroon, 2016). This chapter will therefore study the novel not only through the broader lens of queer theory, but specifically through the lens of transgender theory.

Transing Time

If 'straight time' (Muñoz, 2009, p. 25) is the sociotemporal perpetuation of heteronormative, cisgender privilege and of the associated male/female gender binary, then trans time is the disruption, deconstruction and subversion of that hegemonic system. *The Unintentional Time Traveler* is a fictional example of a process that the transgender scholar, A. Finn Enke, refers to as 'transing' (Enke, 2012, p. 53), 'a practice that takes place within, as well as across, gendered spaces' (Enke, 2012, p. 205). Lucas Crawford, another transgender theorist, describes the transgender body as a 'temporal 'series' of spaces,' and 'as much as [its] characteristics are obviously spatial, so are they temporal' (Crawford, 2016, p. 5).

Moreover, if 'a place,' such as a body, 'is a set of material conditions that endures, then space and time cannot be regarded as discrete categories,' and, consequently, a transgender figure 'suspends the distinction between time and space, as a space that attempts to hold all times, and, as a timekeeper that needs spatial figuring' (Crawford, 2016, p. 5). Jack's time-travelling body transes time precisely because it is a *temporal space* that crosses the illusory boundaries of time and gender. The 'spatial figuring' of Jack's/Jacqueline's changing body within the text is simultaneously a timekeeper that 'attempts to hold all times,' and in doing so, disrupts the linear ordering of the gender binary and of time itself. It is time travel that creates the split between biological sex and gender identity in the novel, by first transporting Jack out of a boy's body and into a girl's.

As Jack/Jacqueline journeys back and forth between contemporary America and Prohibition-era America and between the 'male' and 'female' sex, the self-discovery of their queer, non-binary gender identity is couched in temporal language, i.e. the language of adjustment to different times. The protagonist constantly negotiates and reshapes their gender identity through comparing and re-contextualising their experiences across time. Time travel as a trope in speculative fiction is bound to draw attention to 'the psychic and social environments' in which we live, by creating a 'collective *affect* of "The times we're in"' (Wiegman, 2014, p. 6) and comparing those times to other times. When Jack travels to the past and falls in love with a boy, Jack wonders if, back in the present, that makes 'him' gay, even though, in the woman's body 'she' occupied in the past, 'she' was seemingly straight in 'her' pursuit of a romantic relationship with a boy. Temporarily returning to the present, Jack considers confiding in a gay friend: 'I'd been mean to him because he was gay, and here I was pining away over Lucas. I should tell him' (TUTT, p. 150).

This negotiation of gender identity and sexuality is a familiar transgender narrative, sometimes referred to as transing. In using time travel to journey across gendered spaces, Maroon's novel performs a '*transing* of time' that 'does to […] historicities what *trans* does to […] bodies and to their attendant subjectivities' (Enke, 2012, p. 53). Indeed, the subjective experiences of Jack (in the present) or Jacqueline (in the past) 'exist in a profound complex relative to time' (Enke, 2012, p. 53), and result in a protagonist whose consciousness is in a state of perpetual flux, of internal and external negotiations and adjustments with their bodies, societies and histories. As the following series of quotes illustrates, Jack, who still identifies as a boy at the beginning, is profoundly uncomfortable with occupying a 'female' form and being referred to as female:

'Kentucky hasn't killed anyone for horse stealing in a while, but the penalty's still on the books, young lady.' The word 'lady' sliced into me. (TUTT, p. 33)

'Girl, get over here and make the doctor some coffee.' Girl. I wished they'd stop calling me that. (TUTT, p. 34)

[W]hat was wrong with me that I'd imagined myself as a girl? […] *I must really hate myself to have a hallucination like this*, I thought. (TUTT, p. 34-35)

Jacqueline had a grown woman's body at this point; it was certainly different than I'd ever seen in a dirty magazine. All of these bones were beneath a layer of softness I wasn't used to. […] I worried I was invading someone else's body, even as I wanted to be back in mine. (TUTT, p. 53)

When Jack first awakens in the body of a girl, 'he' finds that body uncomfortable and unfamiliar, but as Jacqueline waking up back in the present, 'she' finds the male body just as, if not more, uncomfortable. The protagonist gradually begins to identify more with Jacqueline's 'female' body:

> I was Jacqueline. That made me grateful; I knew this body at least as well as I knew Jack's. I appreciated her sure-footedness. I enjoyed her gait and the way she cut through space. I felt more centered, as if I was better able to be me. (TUTT, p. 185)

Upon returning to the present, 'Jack' experiences a reverse gender shock. 'Jack' finds it difficult to come to terms with occupying a male body once again, even going so far as to say, 'already my life as a teenage boy seemed like a lie' (TUTT, p. 160). After returning to the past, 'Jacqueline,' rather than resenting going back to a woman's body, proclaims: 'I appreciated not having boy junk to deal with' (TUTT, p. 167). Jack's/Jacqueline's view of the genders and bodies they occupy changes noticeably as the novel progresses.

Jacqueline's body feels increasingly natural to the protagonist as they travel back in time again and again, and, as it turns out, that body also permits Jacqueline—now firmly identifying as she/her—to live in society, albeit Prohibition-era society, with the love of her life, Lucas, with whom she can now get married and have children. The novel ends with Jack *choosing* to live as Jacqueline by choosing to primarily exist in Jacqueline's time and body, although Jacqueline also continues to travel between times and genders, largely to repair the wrongs of history that are within her ability to repair.

Robyn Wiegman argues that a significant portion of queer feminist criticism 'partakes in defining and analyzing the affective in temporal terms and vice versa, producing as much as contesting the atmospheres that reside in cultural domains' (Wiegman, 2014, p. 6). Maroon's use of time travel is a queer means of 'contesting' the atmospheres that reside in past, present, and future cultural domains, domains whose memories, realities or potentialities together map the scope of society's fears and expectations regarding the social constructs of gender and sexuality: 'The queer are the mirror reflecting the heterosexual tribe's fear: being different, being other, and therefore lesser, therefore sub-human, in-human, non-human' (Anzaldúa, 1987, p. 18). Some of these fears are intense enough to qualify as paranoia, as the next section of this chapter discusses.

Pathologisation as Paranoia

The word 'sick' is often used in *The Unintentional Time Traveler* to refer to Jack's epilepsy, which, along with its rather drastic treatment of electric shock, is at first confused by Jack (and Jack's peers) as the reason for 'his' changes in time and gender. Jack only later discovers that this sickness did not by itself cause the time-travelling, and that Jack would have manifested his/her/their time-travelling powers regardless. Nonetheless, for a significant portion of the novel, the notions of illness and queerness intersect, and the uncoupling of those narratives is vital in understanding the protagonist's reclamation of queer agency. Jeannine, Jack's other best friend, initially explains Jack's time travel and apparent gender change away as a sickness, and rationalises that it may be a side effect of Jack's epilepsy:

'Look, you must have seen that box somewhere else, and
then remembered it in your seizure,' said Jeannine.
'I guess so.' I hid my disappointment […] Maybe my
epilepsy was playing with my memory. Or maybe I had
crossed the line into delusional raving lunatic. How would
someone know if they were out of touch with reality,
anyway? Wasn't that like, in the definition? 'I just […] it
seemed so real. Not like a dream.' (TUTT, p. 43)

While Jeannine's suspicion of Jack's experiences is
reasonable to the extent that most would disbelieve someone
claiming to have time-travelled, there is also a definite
element of suspicion regarding Jack's gender identity and
sexuality, not only of his time-travelling. This suspicion
culminates in an instance of sexual assault in which
Jeannine, who thinks she is dating the original, 'male' Jack,
repeatedly attempts to seduce him:

She played with a coil of my hair and I did my best not to
flinch […] 'I can make you feel better,' she said, leaning
in. And before I could say anything, she was kissing me,
pushing through my lips with her tongue.
'Jeannine, Jeannine, stop.' This was not what I wanted or
needed right now. 'What is the issue with you? Shit, Jack.'
'I just […] I don't feel well. Can you just take us to
school?' (TUTT, p. 96-97)

Here, even Jack sees 'his' own inability to react to
Jeannine with the appropriate sexual excitement as a
symptom of illness; he claims not to 'feel well' not only

as an excuse to Jeannine but as an explanation to himself. Thus, the external pathologisation of Jack's gender and sexuality by Jeannine results in Jack being subjected to sexual assault, and his internalised self-pathologisation results in him attempting to normalise and rationalise that assault. Jack even feels guilty that in his failure to respond heterosexually, he is being 'rude' to Jeannine (TUTT, p. 98). Beyond this episode of assault, the broader pathologisation of queerness is also explored through the term 'sick,' which is used by Jack's gay friend, Sanjay, to point out that homosexuality is often treated as a sickness: 'You were the one who said we couldn't be friends, that you didn't really know me, that I was sick. Why would I trust you?' (TUTT, p. 116).

Sickness and queerness only overlap when queerness is pathologised. Sanjay comments on how the AIDS crisis led to the mass pathologisation of gay men: 'Straight people treat gay people like lepers now, tell us it's our fault we're sick' (TUTT, p. 227). The wrongful pathologisation of non-heteronormative sexualities and gender identities has a long and fraught history (Inch, 2016, p. 193), and as a result, 'queer studies in particular has had a distinctive history of intimacy with the paranoid imperative' (Sedgwick, 2003, p. 126).

Pathologisation is itself paranoid, but the paranoid imperative can bleed into the queer resistance of pathologisation, as well. A reparative approach may be more fruitful than a paranoid one in decoding and dismantling the heteronormative agenda of pathologisation. Before exploring how *The Unintentional Time Traveler* exercises a reparative resistance to heteronormative paranoia, I must first explain how the hermeneutics of suspicion applies to pathologisation.

Pathologisation and the Hermeneutics of Suspicion

The pathologisation of queerness can itself be said to be a sort of 'hermeneutics of suspicion' (Sedgwick, 2003, p. 124), in that it *suspects the veracity and validity of queer narratives of self-identification*. Rather than according the queer individual agency, the suspicion of queerness seeks to categorise queer psychology solely as a pathology, to reduce identity to disease, and to assign the labels of sickness, abnormality and perversity to queer identities such as the transgender identity. Just as 'hysteria' was a term once used by the psychiatric community to pathologise femininity and emotionality (Tosh, 2015, p. 112), and just as Freud's 'discredited link […] between paranoia and the repression of same-sex desire' pathologised homosexuality (Wiegman, 2014, p. 9), the false homogenisation of 'the complex interweaving' of the 'multiple narratives' of transgender and genderqueer experiences as a single psychiatric condition, labelled 'gender dysphoria,' has led to the systematic 'pathologization of gender nonconformity' (Tosh, 2015, p. 57). Gender dysphoria is categorised as a mental disorder in the *Diagnostic and Statistical Manual for Mental Disorders*, and is defined as the subjective experience of 'a difference between […] expressed and assigned gender, and which causes significant impairment' (Key, 2014, p. 427). However, this very pathologisation 'can feel degrading and invalidating' for trans individuals who have their 'gender identity, expression, or feelings of dysphoria labelled as a disorder by clinicians' (Carmel, Hopwood and Dickey, 2014, p. 308).

The psychiatrists who aim to treat the mental agony caused by gender dysphoria often sabotage their own efforts through the pathologisation of transness that only results in the further ostracisation and suffering of their patients—a pathologisation that 'is based on the erroneous sex binary, outmoded views of gender, and the misattribution of the causes of distress trans people sometimes experience' (Inch, 2016, p. 193). The dysphoria psychiatrists set out to cure has its source not in the transgender and non-binary gender identities of their patients, but in society's condemnation of them. In *The Unintentional Time Traveler*, it is not now-Jacqueline's shifting gender identity that torments her but the dissonance between her internal gender identity and society's outward expectations, a dissonance that she has internalised and that she experiences as dysphoria. It is this deep internalisation of society's prejudice against gender non-conformity that pains Jacqueline, not the uncomplicated transgender selfhood that exists within her and that society condemns.

> 'You're a grown woman now,' she said, and then she laughed a little. 'And you still insist on wearing men's clothes. Tsk.'
> 'They're comfortable,' I said, happy to tell her anything that wasn't a lie. *Which is weirder*, I wondered, *the grown part or the woman part?* (TUTT, p. 72)

Jacqueline finds 'men's clothes' comfortable because Jack was used to wearing them. This non-binary melding of genders is rendered 'weird' within Jacqueline's mind by her internalisation of the heteronormative bias that clearly demarcates the genders, as evidenced here by the implication that, in the eyes of society, Jacqueline should not be wearing gender non-conforming clothes. This policing of gender performativity within the novel and within society is a type of oppression and erasure. Jacqueline should not be made to feel that, in exercising her own agency regarding her gender performance, she is immediately considered sick and/or freakish, not only by society but by herself— by the binary construct of gender that her psyche has been groomed since childhood to observe with painstaking correctness. Venturing away from the binary norm is subjectively experienced by Jacqueline as a threat to her own survival, and it is this psychological schism between I-am and I-should-be within the genderqueer individual that is at the root of gender dysphoria. Gender dysphoria is a condition inflicted on the transgender individual, not a condition inherent to them. If 'the very 'state' of gender *is* change,' then 'transgender is simply a particularly strong and valuable event of gender—not an exception or aberration to the rule of otherwise static genders' (Crawford, 2016, p. 4). As it is not an aberration, the transgender identity does not require a cure or a correction.

Yet the societal suspicion of queerness is such a fine-toothed comb that it picks up on even the subtlest of visible gender cues, such as Jacqueline's seemingly inappropriate male attire, and instantly discourages those mannerisms before they can form a broader, more dangerous pattern of gender non-conformity. Society's suspicion of Jacqueline marks her as a threat to the status quo, yes, but it also marks the status quo as a threat to Jacqueline. This is such a profoundly internalised threat mentality that Jacqueline sometimes perceives herself as a threat to herself, and perceives her own queerness, her own transness, as an abnormality that must be suppressed or silenced. The perversity of the hermeneutics of suspicion is that it seeks to make queer people complicit in their own oppression. As Ian Parker points out, 'the psychology of perversion is actually itself perverse […] The psychological gaze on gender identity, homosexuality and transgender which finds perversion in those places is actually a perverse gaze that then conceals where the 'abnormality' it pretends to discover really lies' (Parker, 2015, pp. xi-xii). Consequently, the 'social ostracism and victimization of transgender individuals becomes part of the definition of 'gender dysphoria' (Tosh, 2015, p. 91).

As demonstrated by Jacqueline's textual example above, the hermeneutics of suspicion, when applied to a cultural minority such as the queer community with the intent to uncover a fictional evilness, abnormality or perversity in that community, becomes a form of oppression. It is an oppression based on 'doubt about the motives of others' and a 'denial of existence shared by others' (Scott-Baumann, 2009, pp. 7-59), i.e. a denial of an existence shared by queer individuals. Pathologisation is oppression because it frames queer erasure as a type of treatment, as a cure for queerness. This not only erases queer identities but glorifies straight oppressors as healers and rescuers. Under this systemic suspicion of queerness, acts of oppression are morally vindicated, and each apparent successful 'treatment' further bolsters the heteronormative agenda. *The Unintentional*

Time Traveler debunks this agenda by having Jack's gender dysphoria seemingly initially pathologised (and hence deemed 'curable') as epilepsy, but then later revealing that it was not the epilepsy nor its treatment that resulted in Jack's/ Jacqueline's time/gender change. This is a covert means of resistance, however, and does not outright fight fire with fire when it comes to heteronormative paranoia.

Can a queer author fight fire with fire? The answer is no, at least, not effectively, because the 'hermeneutics of suspicion' is double-ended. It creates an action/reaction model of dialogue, which is really no dialogue at all but a backlash in which every action must have an equal and opposite reaction. While oppression must be doubted in order to be resisted, and resistance therefore requires a degree of suspicion—enough, at least, to refuse to believe in the narrative of one's own alleged sickness—too much suspicion can lead to a paranoia that ventures into the territory of 'conspiracy,' as observed by Sedgwick in her essay on hermeneutics. In it, Sedgwick discusses the perceived causes of the AIDS epidemic among the queer community, and how some of the community's conspiracy theories about the origin of AIDS were in themselves paranoid (Sedgwick, 2003, p. 123). Just as society's pathologisation of queerness suspects the authenticity of queer narratives, so do queer narratives, in attempting to resist their own pathologisation, risk going too far in their suspicion and succumbing to the miasma of paranoia that pervades and surrounds heteronormative discourse. This paranoia must itself be unpacked before queer identities can be successfully reclaimed, for if one responds to the heteronormative 'paranoid reading' (Sedgwick, 2003, p.

126) of queer narratives by pursuing a paranoid reading of heteronormativity in return, one might not address the very separatist ideology at the core of the gender binary.

As Wiegman says in quoting Silvan Tomkins, the critical reading (and writing) that results from paranoia has an ' 'impoverishing reliance on a bipolar analytic framework' that sanctions 'unresting critique' by reiterating the very binary relations of subject-object, self-other, and subversive-hegemonic that it is supposedly out to dismantle' (Wiegman, 2014, p. 9). The tyranny of this erroneous binary can only be effectively resisted if the resistance to it is reparative and non-paranoid, for if the resistance to heteronormative paranoia uses the language of suspicion, only further paranoia will result.

Instead, sideways shifts, into and out of multiple interpretive approaches, may be more productive, and time travel as a narratological device certainly offers multiple approaches to the writer and the reader, not only by creating multiple causal (and social) time loops, but also by destabilising the privileging of any temporal perspective above any other. The section below details how time travel generally, and time travel in *The Unintentional Time Traveler* specifically, offers non-paranoid means of resistance to heteronormativity.

Reparative Time Travel

The direct reversal of a paranoid reading can only be another paranoid reading, and that, Sedgwick notes, is the limit of such a 'reflexive and mimetic' reading (Sedgwick, 2003, p. 131). A 'reparative turn' (Wiegman, 2014, p. 7) may be more productive and open to queer potentialities, in that readings of gender identity will then not be limited to a single alternative model intended to resist binary gender, but will be able to generate and accept any and all queer models that may become relevant.

Time travel, as a trope in speculative fiction, is one such reparative approach. Pathologisation is based on privilege—the privileging of straight above gay, cisgender above transgender, and heteronormativity as healthy/normal above non-heteronormativity as unhealthy/abnormal. Thus, resisting the pathologisation of queerness goes hand-in-hand with de-privileging heteronormativity. Time travel is a useful literary device that de-privileges as it de-sequences; the disordering of the past/future sequence calls into question the narrative of privilege altogether, that is, the unequal binary narrative of first or last, winner or loser, human or subhuman. If there can be no overarching order, then how can anything be more privileged or preferred than anything else? As Wiegman says, time travel 'eschew[s] the critical sovereignty of critique in favour of a […] reparative reading [that] revises the political meaning and affective environment of the critical act' (Wiegman, 2014, p. 7). The device of time travel accepts no sovereignty at all, not the sovereignty of past over future, male over female, or heteronormative over non-heteronormative. De-privileging takes no prisoners; in resisting privilege as a world-view, *all* privileges are called into question.

The Unintentional Time Traveler is a queer time travel narrative that refuses to write back at heteronormativity but instead writes through, around and beyond it, in a form of reparative *writing*, thereby restoring agency not only to the non-binary protagonist but to all readers who are willing to engage with the concept of gender identity without paranoia. The novel uses time travel to de-sequence and de-privilege the binary model of gender. Rather than the 'hypervigilance' (Wiegman, 2014, p. 8) of perpetually guarding against heteronormativity, *The Unintentional Time Traveler* instead offers an unforced, open-ended approach to gender identity that allows the protagonist to experience and embody multiple gendered states without privileging any of them.

This reparative approach provides a 'different range' of interpretive possibilities about 'the many ways in which selves and communities succeed in extracting sustenance from the objects of a culture—even of a culture whose avowed desire has often been not to sustain them' (Sedgwick, 2003, pp. 150-151). Non-binary, genderqueer, and transgender commentators need not respond to the paranoia to which they have been subjected by society in general, and by the medical community in particular, with paranoia of their own; indeed, as a text written by a transgender author, *The Unintentional Time Traveler* is overtly non-paranoid and offers a variety of reparative alternatives to the heteronormative paranoia that continues to force a gender binary even upon those, like Jack/Jacqueline, to whom the gender binary does not always apply. The extract below exemplifies the text's reparative approach:

> 'I'm so proud of you, my dear. You're such a wonderful young man.'
> 'Or woman,' said Jackson, grinning on half of his face.
> 'That too,' she said.
> I sighed. (TUTT, p. 237)

This is a crucial moment in *The Unintentional Time
Traveler*, when Jackson, Jacqueline's initially misogynistic
and overwhelmingly heteronormative grandfather, explicitly
accepts her for who she is. Instead of being written with
paranoia, the grizzled character of Jackson is depicted
as redeemable and capable of growth, and is permitted a
degree of complexity and character development that would
not have been available to him had he been villainised.
Jacqueline, who at first bears the brunt of his misogyny, does
not react to him with paranoia, either; instead, she saves his
life by warning him of the cause of his own future death,
and in so doing wins his respect and acceptance. Jackson,
who originally meets the female version of Jacqueline
and assumes (correctly) that she is his granddaughter, is
nonetheless stumped when he discovers that all may not be
as it seems:

'Imagine my surprise when my daughter had a baby boy.'
'Oh, right. About that—'
'It doesn't matter, Jack. I am so grateful I've had all this
time.' (TUTT, p. 236)

In travelling through time, Jacqueline grants *others*
time, too—time to grow, time to learn, and time to redeem
themselves. In an extended reparative metaphor, Jackson,
the epitome of sexist machismo, is the man who Jack
was named after, and it is Jack's renaming of 'himself' as
Jacqueline that finally extricates Jack from 'the temporal
frames of […] reproduction[,] family […] and inheritance'
(Halberstam, 2005, p. 6) that describe straight time. The
novel's transing of time is accomplished via reparative

time travel that resolves Jacqueline's internal gender dysphoria as well as the heteronormative paranoia external to her. This transing liberates not only Jacqueline but those around her, implying that faith in humanity is the antidote to paranoia and that persistence against injustice is the antidote to oppression. The text repairs the relationship between Jackson as a symbol for heteronormative society and Jacqueline as a symbol for the transgender community. It is, quite literally, reparative.

Conclusion

The last line of *The Unintentional Time Traveler* is imbued with confidence, self-ownership and a strong sense of agency. The transgender protagonist, who at the beginning of the novel identified as a boy named Jack, now chooses to identify as a woman: 'I am Jacqueline Leigh Bishop Van Doren, and I can travel through time' (TUTT, p. 246).

The optimism of *The Unintentional Time Traveler* stems not only from how it overcomes pathologisation and paranoia, but from the agency the protagonist reclaims from all that seemingly involuntary time-travelling and body-switching. Jacqueline eventually learns that both can be controlled, and can be undergone voluntarily. The final scene of the book shows Jacqueline choosing to live her life primarily as a woman while still travelling back and forth in time (and gender) as she chooses. There is a marked triumph to her agency, for she has now mastered time *and* gender, and her transformations and journeys through both are entirely of her own volition.

Initially, it seems that Jacqueline's journey of

self-discovery plays into the existing, comfortable-if-disempowering narrative of 'belated discovery,' characterised by Crawford as follows:

> Why must the rupture of transgender so often be tamed into the temporal narrative of belated discovery, when we could imbue it with all the strength and inexplicability of the untimely? If transgender feels like the former, might that be because our feelings are structured by the genres of narrative we've grown to love? (Belated discovery is certainly a familiar and comfortable narrative to us, even if casting ourselves in its plot also entails 'bad' feelings.) (Crawford, 2016, p. 12)

However, in using time travel as a means to destroy the very concept of 'belated,' or indeed of 'late' or 'early,' Maroon makes an authorial decision to extricate the transgender narrative of self-discovery from the linear underpinnings of straight time. Jacqueline discovers herself simultaneously in her past and in her future; such a discovery is atemporal and possesses, as Crawford puts it, 'all the strength and inexplicability of the untimely.'

Jacqueline's 'becoming' deconstructs heteronormativity by disordering the sequencing of the gender binary and by injecting the entropic, chaotic catalyst of free will into the predetermined order of straight time, which, if left to itself, can only draw a straight, uninterrupted line between biological sex at birth and gender identity as an adult. The transformation of Jack into Jacqueline using time travel reconstructs queer normativity through reparative writing instead of combating queer pathologisation through paranoia.

References

Anzaldúa, G. (1987) *Borderlands/La Frontera: The New Mestiza*. San Francisco: Aunt Lute Books.

Carmel, T., Hopwood, R. and Dickey, L.M. (2014) 'Mental Health Concerns,' in Erickson-Schroth, L. (ed.) *Trans Bodies, Trans Selves: A Resource for the Transgender Community*. Oxford: Oxford University Press, pp. 305-334.

Crawford, L. (2016) *Transgender Architectonics: The Shape of Change in Modernist Space*. New York: Routledge.

Enke, A.F. (2012) 'Introduction,' in Enke, A.F. (ed.) *Transfeminist Perspectives: In and Beyond Transgender and Gender Studies*. Philadelphia: Temple University Press, pp. 1-15.

Halberstam, J. (2005) *In a Queer Time and Space*. New York: New York University Press.

Iantaffi, A. (2017) 'Future Directions' in Barker, M., Bouman, W.P. and Richards, C. (eds.) *Genderqueer and Non-Binary Genders*. London: Palgrave Macmillan, pp. 283-296.

Inch, E. (2016) 'Changing Minds: The Psycho-Pathologization of Trans People,' *International Journal of Mental Health*, 45(3), pp. 193-204.

Key, A. (2014) 'Children' in Erickson-Schroth, L. (ed.) *Trans Bodies, Trans Selves: A Resource for the Transgender Community*. Oxford: Oxford University Press, pp. 409-445.

Kuiken, J.S. (2014) 'Interview With Everett Maroon,' *Diversity in YA*, 27 February [online]. Available at: <http://www.diversityinya.com/2014/02/interview-with-everett-maroon/> (Accessed: 18 October 2019).

Markova, I. (2003) *Dialogicality and Social Representations: The Dynamics of Mind*. Cambridge: Cambridge University Press.

Meck, W.H., Penney, T.B. and Schirmer, A. (2016) 'The Socio-Temporal Brain: Connecting People in Time,' *Trends in Cognitive Sciences*, 20(10), pp. 760-772.

Maroon, E. (2016) *Bumbling Into Body Hair: Tales of an Accident-Prone Transsexual*. New Jersey: Lethe Press.
---. (2016) *The Unintentional Time Traveler*. New Jersey: Lethe Press.

Muñoz, J.E. (2009) *Cruising Utopia: The Then and There of Queer Futurity*. New York: New York University Press.

Parker, I. (2015) 'Preface' in Tosh, J., *Perverse Psychology: The pathologization of sexual violence and transgenderism*. New York: Routledge.

Rommetveit, R. (1992) 'Outlines of a dialogically based social-cognitive approach to human cognition and communication' in Wold, A.H. (ed.) *The dialogical alternative: Towards a theory of language and mind*. Vancouver: Scandinavian Press, pp. 19-44.

Scott-Baumann, A. (2009) *Ricoeur and the Hermeneutics of Suspicion*. New York: Continuum Publishing.

Sedgwick, E.K. (2003) *Touching Feeling: Affect, Pedagogy, Performativity*. Durham: Duke University Press.

Simmonds, M. (2012) *Girls/women in inverted commas—facing 'reality' as an XY-female*. PhD Thesis. University of Sussex. Available at: <http://sro.sussex.ac.uk/id/eprint/43431/1/Simmonds,_Margaret.pdf> (Accessed 20 October 2019).

Squiers, A. (2014) *An Introduction to the Social and Political Philosophy of Bertolt Brecht: Revolution and Aesthetics*. Amsterdam: Rodopi.

Tosh, J. (2015) *Perverse Psychology: The pathologization of sexual violence and transgenderism*. New York: Routledge.

Wiegman, R. (2014) 'The times we're in: Queer feminist criticism and the reparative "turn" ,' *Feminist Theory*, 15(1), pp. 4-25.

Zerubavel, E. (1985) *Hidden Rhythms: Schedules and Calendars in Social Life*. Berkeley: California University Press.

CONCLUSION

A Collective Temporal Distortion

The time is out of joint—O cursed sprite,
That ever I was born to set it right!
— William Shakespeare, *Hamlet*.

Queer Potentialities

The queer potentialities within the primary texts studied in this book are not simply nascent attributes of the texts, hiding coyly between the lines and waiting passively to be discovered. Instead, they actively invite a queer reading of the texts by deliberately disrupting, deconstructing and destabilising the heteronormative notion of binary gender. A queer reading is hence also an active endeavour, through which the reader co-creates and, in a sense, co-authors a queer narrative and a queer worldview—a worldview not limited to the texts themselves but to a reading of, and participation in, the broader world itself.

> [A] queer reading is performative in itself and [...] is, in the long run, less about content [...] than about worldview. Queer readings are informed by a desire to understand the text both in terms of its potential for

representing dissident sexual subjectivities outside of a Cartesian understanding of the subject and in terms of the text's engagement with a specific historico-cultural understanding of dissident sexualities and of the place of such sexualities within the sex/gender system that regulates and constructs normative—and thus also non-normative—ways of being-in-the-world as a sexed and sexual object. (Pearson, 2008, p. 34)

Each of the time travel stories interpreted in this book are proactively 'dissident,' performing queer writing as well as inviting queer reading, and challenging heteronormative 'ways of being-in-the-world as a sexed and sexual object.' Through time travel, the primary texts 'recast' the idea of gender 'within a zone of temporality we can gesture toward as that of ongoingness, getting by, and living on, where the structural inequalities are dispersed [and] the pacing of their experience [is] intermittent' (Berlant, 2007, pp. 758-759). The *making intermittent* of heteronormativity—which is otherwise a perpetual, uninterrupted linear timeline and is an inescapable narrative that forcefully surrounds, contextualises and interprets all our gender identities and sexual identities—simultaneously 'disperse[s]' the 'structural inequalities' of binary gender. Through the interruption of straight time, the fictional trope of time travel lends the texts' protagonists, and us, 'a kind of interruptive agency that aspires to detach from a condition' (Berlant, 2007, pp. 758-759), the condition here being labelled as a binary entity within a binary system.

In this book, I have demonstrated how three works of speculative fiction employ various methods in dismantling the gender binary through time travel. Virginia Woolf's

Orlando artfully transitions from straight time to queer time and naturalises the process of gender change through a transformative sleep; Robert A. Heinlein's story 'All You Zombies' queers reproduction and subverts gendered language registers; and Everett Maroon's *The Unintentional Time Traveler* engages with the fraught history of transgender pathologisation through reparative writing. All three narratives interrogate the male/female heteronormative gender binary, and hint, textually or subtextually, at alternative gender identities and queer potentialities.

These 'potentialities,' unlike mere possibilities, 'have a temporality that is not in the present but, more nearly, in the horizon' (Muñoz, 2009, p. 99). Each of the primary texts I have studied provide a palpable sense of the nearness of queerness, a glimpse into the future of gender alterity, and they do so by taking the reader from the seemingly straight, heteronormative starting point of a cisgender male protagonist to a character with a more complex, nuanced and non-binary gender identity. The implication of these texts—their *potentiality*—is perhaps queerer than the texts themselves; it is the implication that we are all, even those of us who think we identify according to a binary model of gender, only a step away from queerness, like the protagonists who are made to discover, through circumstance, that their own gender is not as binary as they once thought it was, and that, as a result, their sexuality is not as straight as they thought it was, either. As the narrator of *Orlando* says:

> Different though the sexes are, they intermix. In every human being a vacillation from one sex to the other

takes place, and often it is only the clothes that keep the male or female likeness, while underneath the sex is the very opposite of what it is above. Of the complications and confusions which thus result everyone has had experience... (*Orlando*, ch. 4 par. 51)

The above quote comments on the human psyche's enduring resistance to binaries, including the gender binary, despite society's insistence upon them. Texts like *Orlando*, 'All You Zombies' and *The Unintentional Time Traveler* all invite the reader to question the gender binary and to explore their own gender identity. The primary texts I have studied in this book suggest 'that we are interpellated by our own reading practices, that we become who we are by the ways in which we interpret the world, indeed that seeing the world queerly makes us queer' (Pearson, 2008, p. 90). Their collective deconstruction of the gender binary is an invitation to read the texts, the world, and ourselves 'queerly,' to conceive of and participate in a more non-binary version of reality.

The Non-Binary Movement

Given the number of works of speculative fiction belonging to the subgenre of gender-change-through-time-travel, such as Glasshouse by Charles Stross (2007), *Chronin: The Knife At Your Back* by Alison Wilgus (2019) and *This Is How You Lose the Time War* by Max Gladstone and Amal El-Mohtar (2019), and the even larger number of works engaging more generally with gender identity through time, such as Marge Piercy's *Woman on the Edge of Time* (1976), James Alan

Gardner's *Commitment Hour* (1998) and Derek Beaven's *Newton's Niece* (1999), it is clear that speculative fiction has long been moving away from a default assumption of the gender binary and towards a questioning of that binary. Lauren Lacey, a scholar of women's speculative fiction, observes that '[t]here is a movement away from binary thinking and toward hybrid beasts, open-ended quests, and new tales' (2014, p. 63). This movement towards the non-binary is increasingly prevalent in today's popular culture:

> In recent years, nonbinary gender identities and expressions have enjoyed heightened popularity and visibility in popular culture. This is likely due to three factors: First, the Internet and social media in particular have extended the reach and impact of content dissemination. Second, greater numbers of nonbinary people are coming out, and in many cases, they are coming out at younger ages than previous generations. Finally, several celebrities have allied themselves with nonbinary politics or come out as nonbinary themselves. (McNabb, 2018, p. 55)

Social change and literary change go hand-in-hand, and the burgeoning acceptance of, and curiosity about, queer and/or non-binary identities in society has directly resulted in the popularisation of literature that challenges the gender binary. Popular culture, be it through speculative fiction or through television shows like *Star Trek* (McNabb, 2018, p. 55) and *Doctor Who* (Cole, 2018), is depicting gender change and non-binary gender identities at a greater rate than ever before. Brit Mandelo, editor of *Beyond Binary: Genderqueer and Sexually Fluid Speculative Fiction* (2012), states in the introduction to the anthology that:

Non-binary identities and expressions are often
marginalized; our voices are silenced, our identities
are effaced, and our stories go untold. This has begun
to change with the publication of more and more
genderqueer, bisexual, pansexual, and otherwise non-
binary narratives... (Mandelo, 2012, p. 2)

There is, therefore, a consensus among scholars and
editors of speculative fiction that there is a push towards the
non-binary. The unending Möbius strip of life-influencing-
art and art-influencing-life is just as non-binary as the '[s]
nake that eats its own tail, forever without end' (AYZ, par.
25) from Heinlein's short story, 'All You Zombies.' The
more common the representations of the queer and the non-
binary in fiction, the more visibility these identities have in
real life; 'queer representation' in literature and the media is
directly linked to the 'visibility of queer life' (Peele, 2007,
p. 5) and its wider acceptance. The creative momentum
behind this non-binary movement is future-facing and full
of potential, or, as José Esteban Muñoz would say:

We must vacate the here and now for a then and there.
Individual transports are insufficient. We need to engage
in a collective temporal distortion. We need to step out
of the rigid conceptualisation that is a straight present.
(Muñoz, 2009, p. 185)

The three primary texts that are the focus of this book are
also part of this non-binary movement. Indeed, the growing
speculative fiction subgenre of gender-change-through-time-
travel is, quite literally, 'a collective temporal distortion' that
invites the reader to 'step out of the rigid conceptualisation'

of a straight, cisgender, binary understanding of gender. In isolation, each text engages with an individual reader and achieves an '[i]ndividual transport,' but collectively, the subgenre can engage with society, and can challenge the gender binary on a larger scale.

References

Berlant, L. (2007) 'Slow Death (Sovereignty, Obesity, Lateral Agency),' *Critical Inquiry*, 33(4), pp. 754-780.

Cole, S. (2018) *Doctor Who: Combat Magicks*. London: BBC Books.

Lacey, L.J. (2014) *The Past That Might Have Been, the Future That May Come: Women Writing Fantastic Fiction, 1960s to the Present*. North Carolina: McFarland & Company.

Mandelo, B. (2012) *Beyond Binary: Genderqueer and Sexually Fluid Speculative Fiction*. New Jersey: Lethe Press.

McNabb, C. (2018) *Nonbinary Gender Identities: History, Culture, Resources*. Lanham: Rowman & Littlefield.

Muñoz, J.E. (2009) *Cruising Utopia: The Then and There of Queer Futurity*. New York: New York University Press.

Pearson, W.G. (2008) 'Alien Cryptographies: The View From Queer' in Pearson, W.G., Gordon, J. and Hollinger, V. (eds.) *Queer Universes: Sexualities in Science Fiction*. Liverpool: Liverpool University Press, pp. 14-38.

Peele, T. (2007) 'Introduction: Popular Culture, Queer Culture' in Peele, T. (ed.) *Queer Popular Culture: Literature, Media, Film, and Television*. London: Palgrave Macmillan, pp. 1-8.

Shakespeare, W. (1998) *Hamlet*. New York: Signet Classics.

Woolf, V. (2015) *Orlando: A Biography. EBooks@Adelaide* [online]. Available at: <https://ebooks.adelaide.edu.au/w/woolf/virginia/w91o/complete.html> (Accessed 26 October 2019).

Acknowledgements

I would like to thank my Masters supervisor, Associate Professor Jane Messer, for her guidance and her generosity of spirit. It was the thesis I wrote under her supervision that I eventually converted into this book. Additionally, I am grateful to Macquarie University for funding my research with a scholarship so that I could focus wholly on my thesis.

I would also like to thank my family for standing by me throughout the writing process. Without Tat's, Sid's and my parents' loving support, I wouldn't have been able to complete this book!

And, last but certainly not least, I would like to thank Francesca T. Barbini of Luna Press Publishing for giving this rather niche book a chance.

Thank you all!